2004 Annual Report

*Migratory Bird
Conservation Commission*

75 Years

Of preserving waterfowl habitat.

The Migratory Bird Conservation Commission

Section 2 of the Migratory Bird Conservation Act of February 18, 1929 (Act), as amended, established the Migratory Bird Conservation Commission.

Section 2. A Commission to be known as the Migratory Bird Conservation Commission, consisting of the Secretary of the Interior, as Chairman; the Administrator of the Environmental Protection Agency; the Secretary of Agriculture; two Members of the Senate, to be selected by the President of the Senate; and two Members of the House of Representatives, to be selected by the Speaker, is created and authorized to consider and pass upon any area of land, water, or land and water that may be recommended by the Secretary of the Interior for purchase or rental under this Act and to fix the price or prices at which such area may be purchased or rented; and no purchase or rental shall be made of any such area until it has been duly approved for purchase or rental by said Commission.

Any Member of the House of Representatives who is a member of the Commission, if reelected to the succeeding Congress, may serve on the Commission notwithstanding the expiration of a Congress. Any vacancy on the Commission shall be filled in the same manner as the original appointment. The ranking officer of the branch or department of a State to which is committed the administration of its game laws, or his authorized representative, shall be a member ex officio of said Commission for the purpose of considering and voting on all questions relating to the acquisition, under said sections, of areas in his State. For purposes of said sections, the purchase or rental of any area of land, water, or land and water includes the purchase or rental of any interest in any such area of land, water, or land and water.

Membership

Hon. Gale Norton
Secretary of the Interior, Chairman

Hon. Ann M. Veneman
Secretary of Agriculture

Hon. Michael O. Leavitt
Administrator, Environmental Protection Agency

Hon. John B. Breaux
Senator from Louisiana

Hon. Thad Cochran
Senator from Mississippi

Hon. John D. Dingell
Representative from Michigan

Hon. Curt Weldon
Representative from Pennsylvania

A. Eric Alvarez
Secretary to the Commission
Telephone: 703/358 1716

Report of the Migratory Bird Conservation Commission for the Fiscal Year 2004

*Front Cover: 2004-2005 Duck Stamp Artwork—Redheads
(Painting by Scot Storm)*

Approvals During Fiscal Year 2004

In Fiscal Year 2004, the Migratory Bird Conservation Commission approved the acquisition boundary at two national wildlife refuges. The first refuge, totaling 98,029 acres, is the Tensas River NWR in Madison and Tensas Parishes, Louisiana. It was authorized by Public Law 96-285 and was established on February 5, 1985. The second refuge, totaling 24,000 acres, is the Canaan Valley National Wildlife Refuge in Tucker County, West Virginia. It was established in August 1994, as our nation's 500th refuge. The Commission approved boundary additions, totaling 27,988 acres, to eleven refuges that were previously approved by the Commission. The Commission also approved the purchase price of 905 acres at four refuges.

Area Approvals—New Areas

State	Area	New Area Acres
Louisiana	Tensas River NWR	98,029
West Virginia	Canaan Valley NWR	24,000
Total		**122,029**

Area Approvals—Additions

State	Area	Addition Acres
Louisiana	Red River NWR	14,397
Maine	Lake Umbagog NWR	466
Maine	Rachel Carson NWR	275
Michigan	Detroit River NWR	410
New Hampshire	Silvio O. Conte NWR	5,103
New Jersey	Cape May NWR	1,632
New Jersey	Edwin B. Forsythe NWR	850
Texas	Anahuac NWR	43
Texas	McFaddin NWR	2,681
Texas	San Bernard NWR	1,906
Texas	Trinity River NWR	225
Total		**27,988**

Price Approvals

State	Area	Price Approval Acres
Louisiana	Lake Ophelia WMA	6
Louisiana	Red River NWR	320
New Jersey	Wallkill River NWR	93
West Virginia	Canaan Valley NWR	486
Total		**905**

The Migratory Bird Conservation Fund

The Migratory Bird Conservation Fund provides the Department of the Interior with monies to acquire migratory bird habitat. There are four major sources of money for the Fund. The most well-known source is the revenue received from the sale of Migratory Bird Hunting and Conservation Stamps, commonly known as Duck Stamps, as provided for under the Migratory Bird Hunting and Conservation Stamp Act of March 18, 1934, as amended. The other three major sources include appropriations authorized by the Wetlands Loan Act of October 4, 1961, as amended; import duties collected on arms and ammunition; and receipts from the sale of refuge admission permits as provided for in the Emergency Wetlands Resources Act of 1986. The Fund is further supplemented by receipts from the sale of products from refuge lands and rights-of-ways across national wildlife refuges, the disposal of refuge lands, and reverted Federal Aid funds.

Two land acquisition programs are financed from the Migratory Bird Conservation Fund. The first purchases major areas for migratory birds under the authority of the Migratory Bird Conservation Act. Lands acquired through this program are considered and approved by the Migratory Bird Conservation Commission. The second program acquires small natural wetlands and associated uplands located mainly in the Prairie Pothole Region of the upper Midwest. These lands, known as Waterfowl Production Areas, are acquired under the authority of the Migratory Bird Hunting and Conservation Stamp Act and do not require approval from the Commission.

During Fiscal Year 2004, the Department of the Interior obligated a total of $17,399,900 for the acquisition of land and interests in land totaling 25,094 acres in major migratory bird conservation areas. An additional $15,928,161 was obligated for projects in Waterfowl Production Areas totaling 45,532 acres.

A total of $46,473,958 was available for obligation from the Migratory Bird Conservation Fund during Fiscal Year 2004. Obligations for all Migratory Bird Conservation Fund land acquisition functions during the fiscal year totaled $44,792,966 (of which $515,092 was from prior year recoveries). The total obligations equal 96 percent of the available funds.

Summary of FY 2004 MBCF Land Acquisitions

Land Contracted for Purchase or Lease

National Wildlife Refuges: Purchase

State	Area	Acres
Arkansas	Cache River	518
California	Grasslands WMA	1,905
California	Grasslands WMA (easements)	1,094
California	North Central Valley WMA (easements)	805
California	Willow Creek/Lurline WMA (easements)	99
Louisiana	Lake Ophelia	6
Louisiana	Red River	1,402
Louisiana	Tensas River	1,976
Michigan	Detroit River	816
New Hampshire	Lake Umbagog	816
New Hampshire	Silvio O. Conte	558
New Jersey	Cape May	47
New Jersey	Edwin B. Forsythe	213
New York	Wallkill River	45
North Carolina	Roanoke River	1,585
Tennessee	Chickasaw	254
Texas	Anahuac	43
Texas	McFadden	2,681
Texas	San Bernard	1,245
Texas	Trinity River	245
West Virginia	Canaan Valley	642
Total		**15,466**

National Wildlife Refuges: Lease

State	Area	Acres
Colorado	Browns Park	636
Louisiana	Lacassine	653
Louisiana	Upper Ouachita	3,217
Mississippi	Dahomey	260
Mississippi	Panther Swamp	640
Mississippi	St. Catherine Creek	502
Montana	Lost Trail	240
Utah	Ouray	2,693
Wyoming	Cokeville Meadows	787
Total		**9,628**

Waterfowl Production Areas

State	Types of Acquisition	Acres
Iowa	Fee	834
Minnesota	Fee	1,127
Minnesota	Easement	3,192
Montana	Easement	2,730
Montana	Lease	1,400
North Dakota	Fee	788
North Dakota	Easement	4,483
South Dakota	Fee	15
South Dakota	Easement	30,749
Wisconsin	Fee	214
Total		**45,532**
Grand Total		**70,626**

New National Wildlife Refuge Boundary Approvals

In Fiscal Year 2004, the Migratory Bird Conservation Commission approved the acquisition boundary of two new refuges, Tensas River National Wildlife Refuge in Madison and Tensas Parishes, Louisiana and Canaan Valley National Wildlife Refuge Tucker County, West Virginia. The Commission also approved the acquisition boundary of eleven national wildlife refuges that were previously established: Anahuac National Wildlife Refuge in Galveston County, Texas; Cape May National Wildlife Refuge in Cape May County, New Jersey; Detroit River International Wildlife Refuge in Wayne County, Michigan; Edwin B. Forsythe National Wildlife Refuge in Atlantic, Burlington, and Ocean Counties, New Jersey; Lake Umbagog National Wildlife Refuge in Oxford County, Maine; McFaddin National Wildlife Refuge in Galveston County, Texas; Rachel Carson National Wildlife Refuge in York and Cumberland Counties, Maine; Red River National Wildlife Refuge in Caddo, Bossier, Desoto, Red River and Natchitoches Parishes, Louisiana; San Bernard National Wildlife Refuge in Brazoria County, Texas; Silvio O. Conte National Fish and Wildlife Refuge, New Hampshire and, Trinity River National Wildlife Refuge in Liberty County, Texas.

Tensas River
National Wildlife Refuge

*Madison and Tensas Parishes,
Louisiana*

Tensas River National Wildlife Refuge was established on June 28, 1980, by Public Law 96-285, to preserve the largest remaining privately owned bottomland hardwood forest tract in the Lower Mississippi River Delta. Tensas River NWR is one of a network of refuges established to preserve and restore habitats for native wildlife and migratory birds.

The purpose of Tensas River NWR is to preserve and restore bottomland hardwood forest and other natural habitats. In addition to the numerous species of mammals and birds, the bottomland hardwood forests on the refuge provide habitat for the Louisiana Black Bear, a Federally-listed threatened species. The backwater sloughs, lakes, and bayous provide habitat for a great diversity of aquatic life including fish, reptiles, amphibians, mollusks, and crustaceans. This refuge provides wintering habitat for mallards, pintails, gadwall, wigeon, green-winged teal, wood ducks, and contributes to the goals of the North American Waterfowl Management Plan. Reforestation and restoration of native habitats will benefit resident and migratory waterfowl as well a wide array of other species. In addition, the refuge offers recreational, research, and educational opportunities.

The Commission approved the 98,029 acre refuge boundary and also gave price approval for a 10,948 acre tract on September 8, 2004.

Tensas River National Wildlife Refuge
Madison and Tensas Parishes, Louisiana

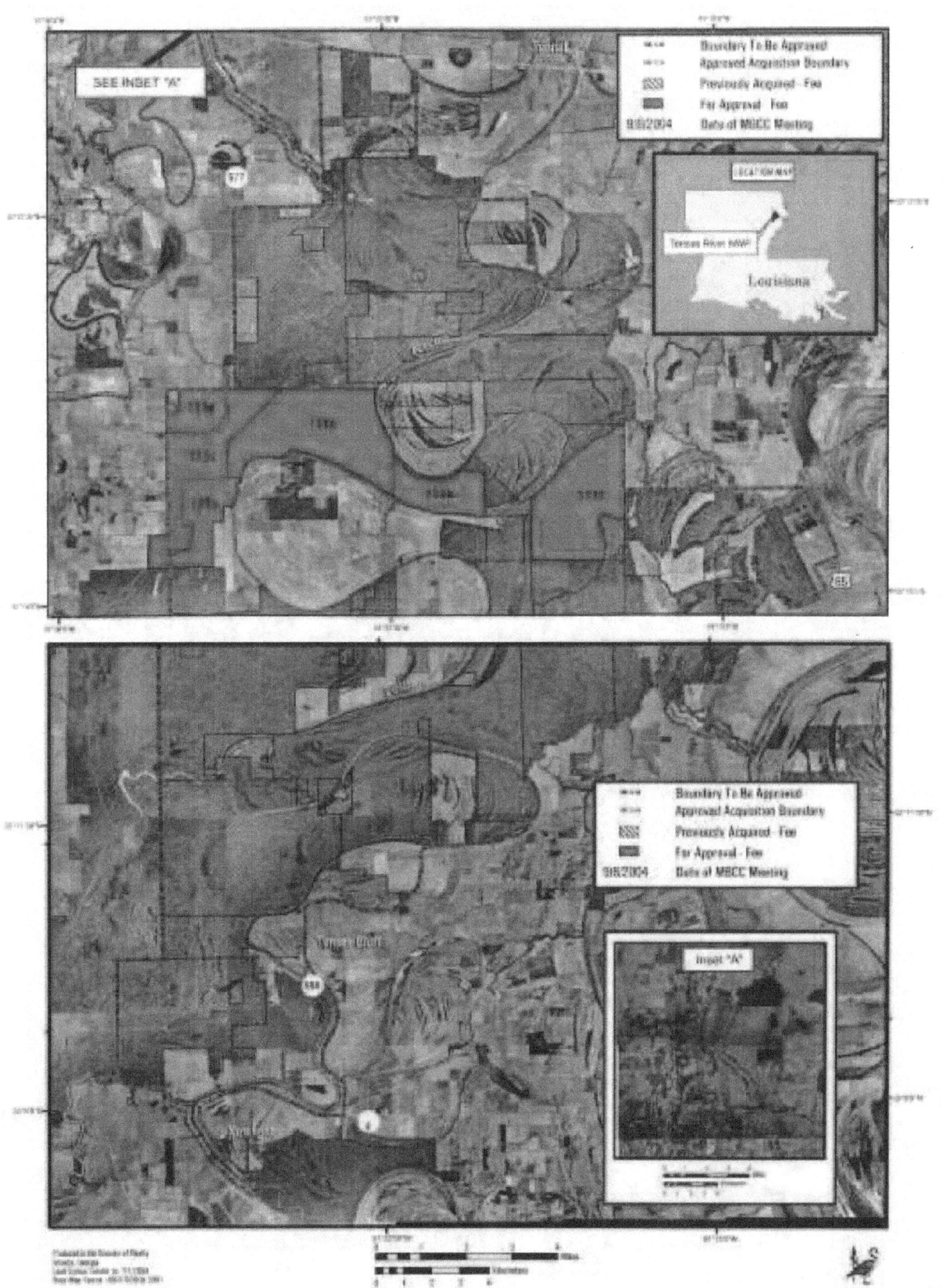

Canaan Valley National Wildlife Refuge
Tucker County, West Virginia

Canaan Valley National Wildlife Refuge is the result of efforts by numerous conservation groups and other partners working with the U.S. Fish and Wildlife Service to protect this unique ecosystem. These efforts commenced in 1961 with a study of the Valley's nationally significant wetlands and wildlife habitats, and culminated with the establishment of the Canaan Valley NWR, our nation's 500th refuge, in August of 1994. The refuge boundary includes 24,000 acres; approximately 15,242 acres have been acquired utilizing funds from the Land and Water Conservation Fund. Land use changes continue to threaten this unique and fragile area.

The habitats in the valley support diverse wildlife populations including important waterfowl and other high priority migratory birds. The wetlands are important for breeding by mallard and wood duck and as stopover habitat for a number of duck and geese species during spring and fall migration, including the American black duck. A number of springs along the Blackwater River and its tributaries stay open during the winter and provide wintering habitat for waterfowl.

Canaan Valley is located in some of the most rugged and mountainous terrain in West Virginia, it is 14 miles long and 2 to 4 miles wide. The average elevation of the valley floor is 3,200 feet, making it the highest valley of its size east of the Rocky Mountains. In 1974, the Secretary of the Interior designated the northern part of the valley, 15,400 acres, as a National Natural Landmark.

The Commission approved the 24,000 acre refuge boundary and also gave price approval for a 156 acre tract on June 9, 2004.

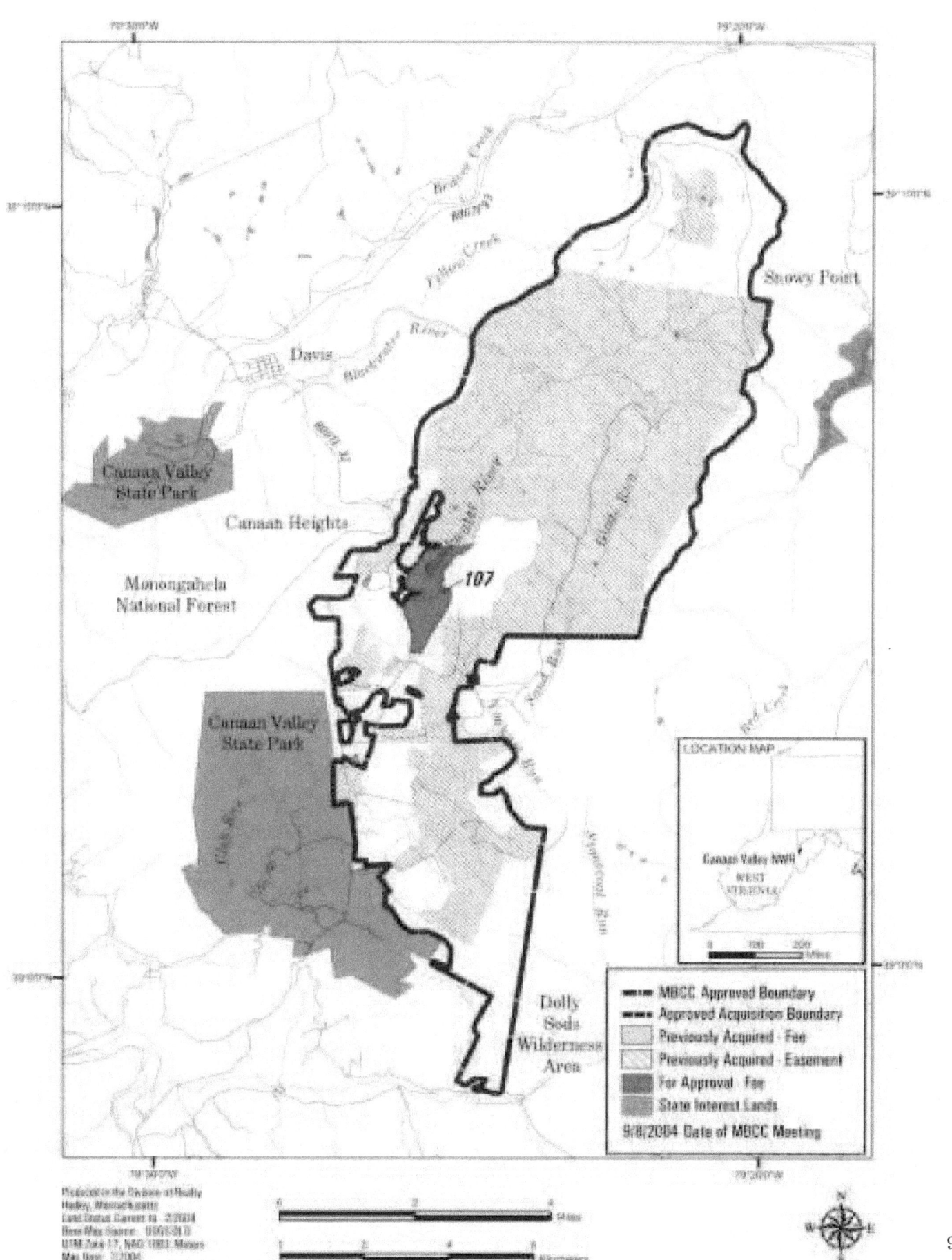

Anahuac National Wildlife Refuge
Galveston County, Texas

On February 27, 1962, the Migratory Bird Conservation Commission approved the establishment of Anahuac National Wildlife Refuge (Refuge). Following the initial approvals, the Commission approved the acquisition of an additional 20,088 acres with monies from the Migratory Bird Conservation Fund. Another 4,372 acres have been acquired with Land and Water Conservation Funds, through donations, and road easements.

The marsh and prairie provide feeding and resting habitat to Central Flyway waterfowl migrating through and wintering on the upper Texas Coast. Twenty-three species of ducks and four species of geese have been observed on or adjacent to this site. The marsh and neighboring uplands provide nesting and brooding areas for the mottled duck. This area is within the North American Waterfowl Management Plan's (NAWMP) Gulf Coast Joint Venture-Chenier Plain Initiative (GCJV-CPI), and has been identified as a high priority for acquisition.

The Commission approved the 43 acre refuge boundary addition and price approval on June 9, 2004.

Anahuac National Wildlife Refuge
Galveston County, Texas

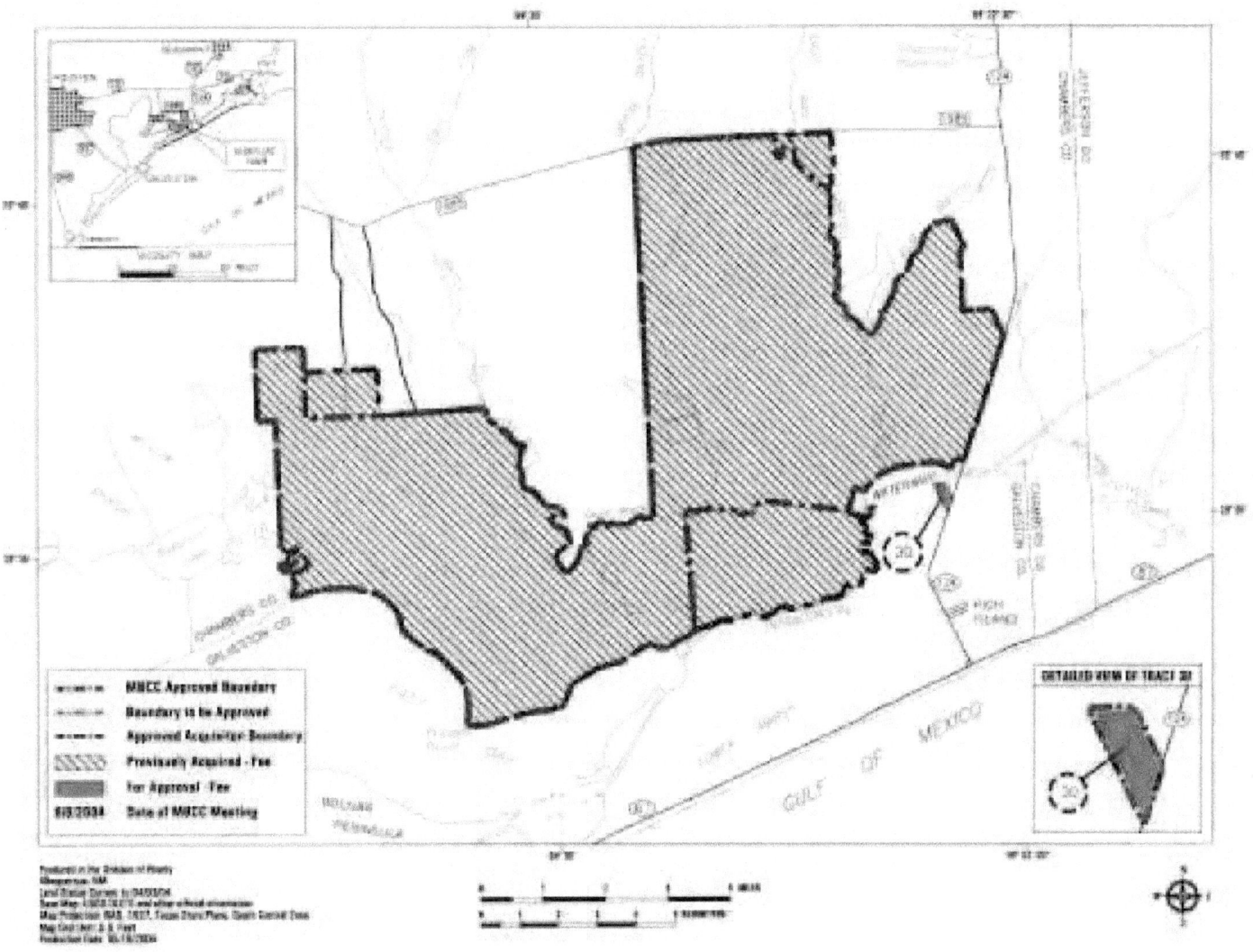

Cape May National Wildlife Refuge
Cape May County, New Jersey

Cape May National Wildlife Refuge was originally approved by the Migratory Bird Conservation Commission on May 9, 1989. To date, 4,416 acres have been acquired with monies from the Migratory Bird Conservation Fund and an additional 6,125 acres have been acquired using the Land and Water Conservation Fund. Two years ago the Coast Guard transferred 625 acres at no cost to the Service. The Refuge is located in Cape May County, New Jersey, and is made up of two divisions. The Delaware Bay Division is along a five-mile stretch of Delaware Bay, and includes the former Coast Guard station and adjacent lands locally known as îTwo Mile Beachî just north of the Cape May Canal on the Atlantic Ocean, and the Great Cedar Swamp Division acres that includes the headwaters of two tidal rivers.

The coastal wetlands of New Jersey, especially the Delaware Bay marshes, annually winter 30 to 40 percent of the Atlantic Flyway Black Duck population. The Black Duck relies heavily on small tidal and fresh water creeks within these areas because they remain ice-free during most of the winter season. This area also provides migration habitat for millions of other birds that are funneled through the Cape May peninsula during migrational periods.

The Commission approved the 1,632 acre refuge boundary addition and price approval for a 47 acre tract on March 3, 2004.

Cape May National Wildlife Refuge
Cape May County, New Jersey

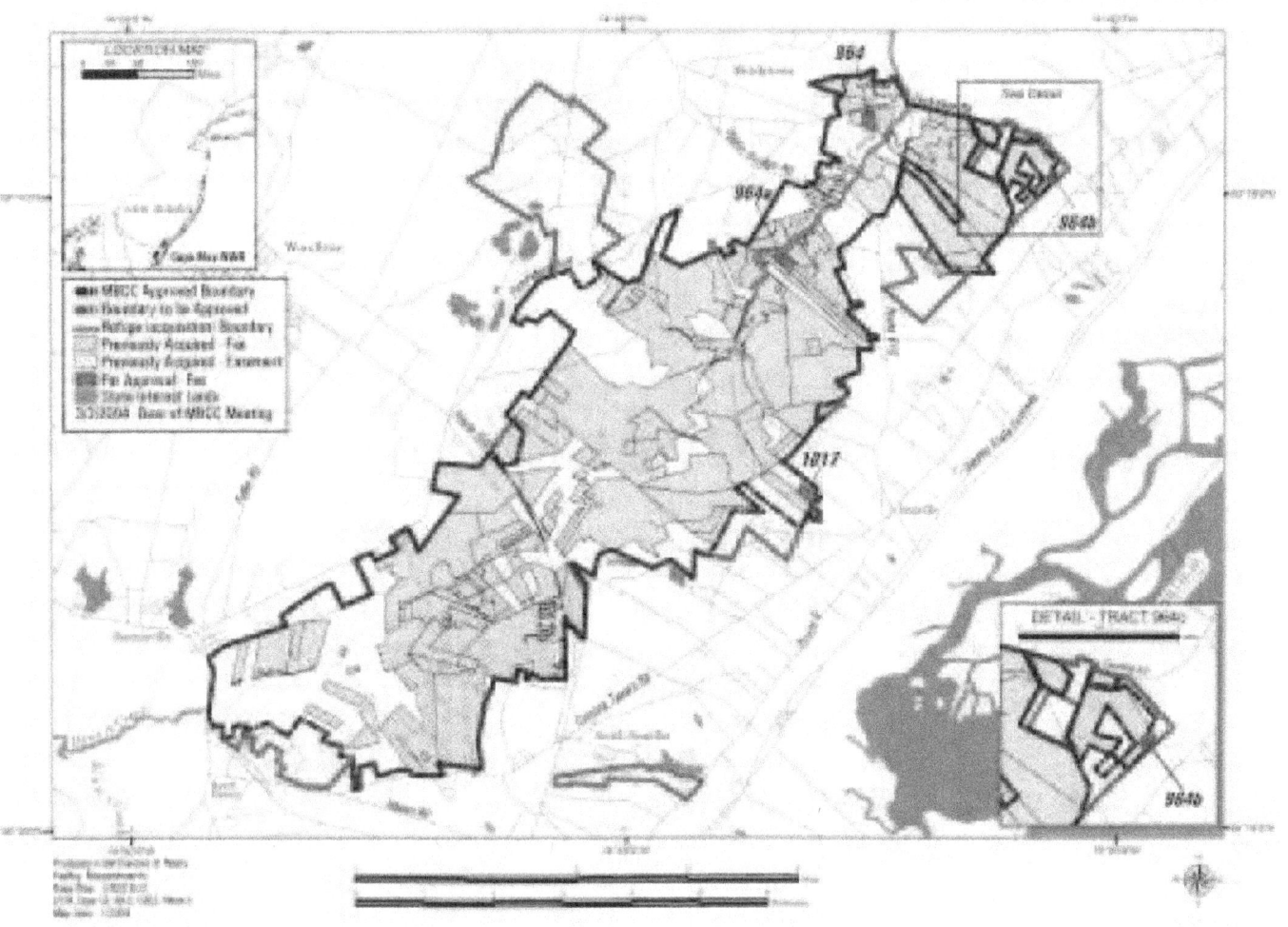

Detroit River International Wildlife Refuge
Wayne County, Michigan

The Detroit River International Wildlife
Refuge (Refuge) was established on
December 21, 2001 by P.L. 107-91
(H.R.1230) Detroit River International
Wildlife Refuge Establishment Act and
expanded on May 19, 2003, Public Law
108-23, the Ottawa National Wildlife
refuge complex Expansion and Detroit
River International Wildlife Refuge
Expansion Act. The first international
refuge in North America, will conserve,
protect and restore habitat for 29 species
of waterfowl, 65 kinds of fish and 300
species of migratory birds on more than
5,000 acres along the lower Detroit River
in Michigan and Canada. The refuge was
approved by the Migratory Bird
Conservation Commission on June 25,
2003.

The refuge includes islands, coastal
wetlands, marshes, shoals and riverfront
lands along 18 miles of the Lower Detroit
River from Zug Island south along
western Lake Erie to the southern
boundary of Sterling State Park in
Monroe County, Michigan. The refuge
also includes Mud Island, Calf Island, and
Grassy Island, lands formerly managed
by the Service as Wyandotte National
Wildlife Refuge. The 326-acre Wyandotte
NWR was re-designated as part of the
refuge.

The Commission approved the 409-acre
refuge boundary addition and price
approval on June 9, 2004.

Detroit River International Wildlife Refuge
Wayne County, Michigan

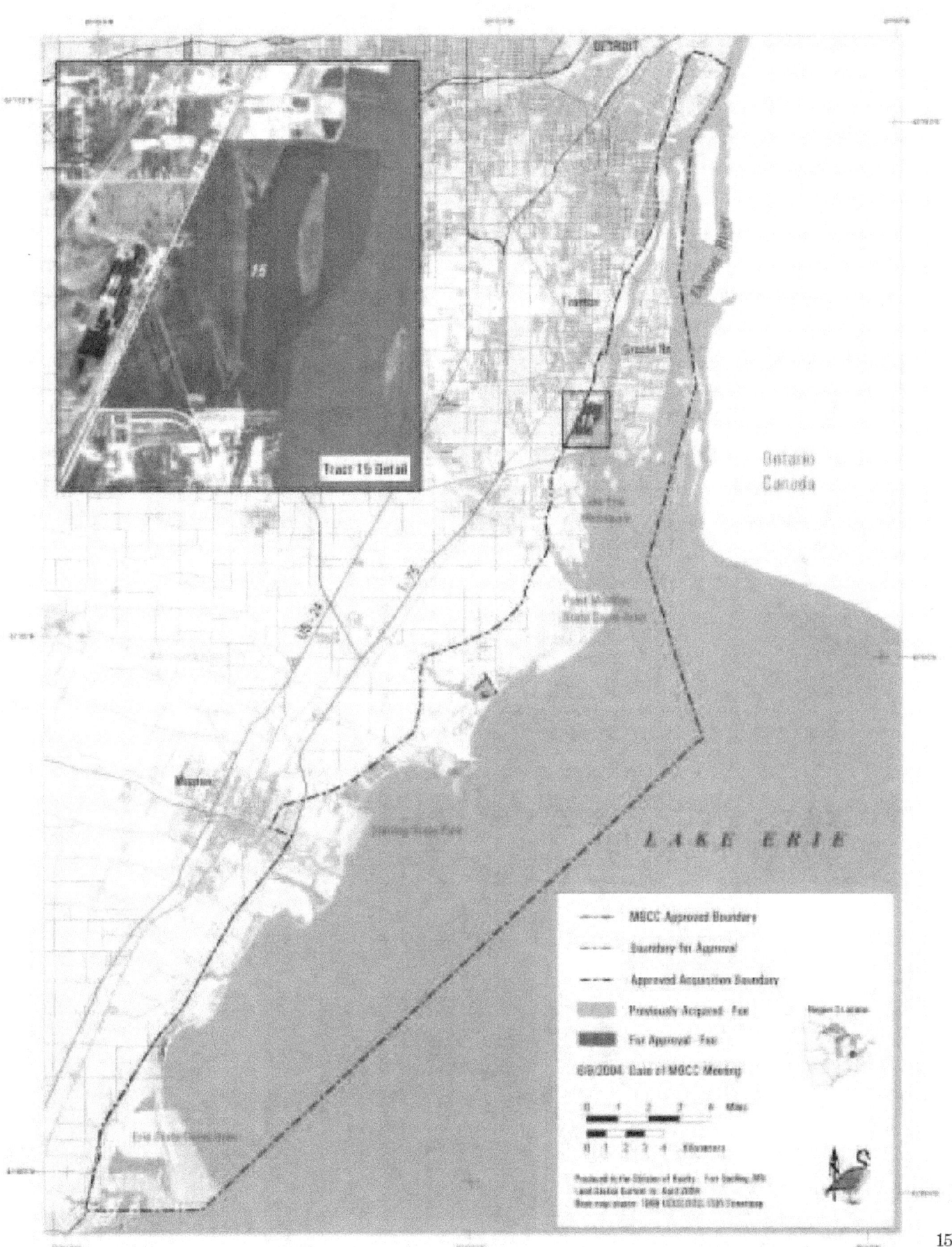

Edwin B. Forsythe National Wildlife Refuge
Atlantic, Burlington and Ocean Counties, New Jersey

Edwin B. Forsythe National Wildlife Refuge is the result of a Congressional action in 1984 which united the Brigantine and Barnegat National Wildlife Refuges in honor of the late Congressman. To date 39,178 acres have been acquired with Migratory Bird Conservation Funds, 2,967 acres have been acquired with Land and Water Conservation Funds, and an additional 3,943 acres have been acquired by easement and donation. Acquired Refuge lands encompass 46,088 acres of predominantly estuarine marsh habitat that grades into brackish and fresh water wetlands, including some stands of Atlantic white cedar. The barrier islands ecosystem and the upland forest and fields increases the biodiversity area of the Refuge.

The Refuge provides the necessary breeding habitat, food, cover, travel corridors and wintering habitat for the survival of those species of waterfowl that utilize the Atlantic Flyway. It is also the first major estuarine area encountered by waterfowl in the United States as they migrate southward from the small glaciated wetlands of the Northeast. These coastal wetlands annually winter approximately 35% of the entire Atlantic Flyway population of American black ducks and 70% of the Flyway's Atlantic brant population. The northern end of the Refuge is approximately 65 miles south of New York City and the southern end is only six miles north of Atlantic City. Residential and commercial development pressure, though somewhat abated from its rampant pace at the end of the last decade, shows no sign of reversal. Marsh destruction has been reduced by the passage of the New Jersey Wetlands Act of 1970 and the State's assertion of its riparian claim. There is, however, a renewed assault by development on marginal areas as wetlands protection legislation is being challenged, and manpower constraints make enforcement ineffective.

The Commission approved the 850 acre refuge boundary addition and price approval for a 28 acre tract on September 8, 2004.

Edwin B. Forsythe National Wildlife Refuge
Atlantic, Burlington and Ocean Counties, New Jersey

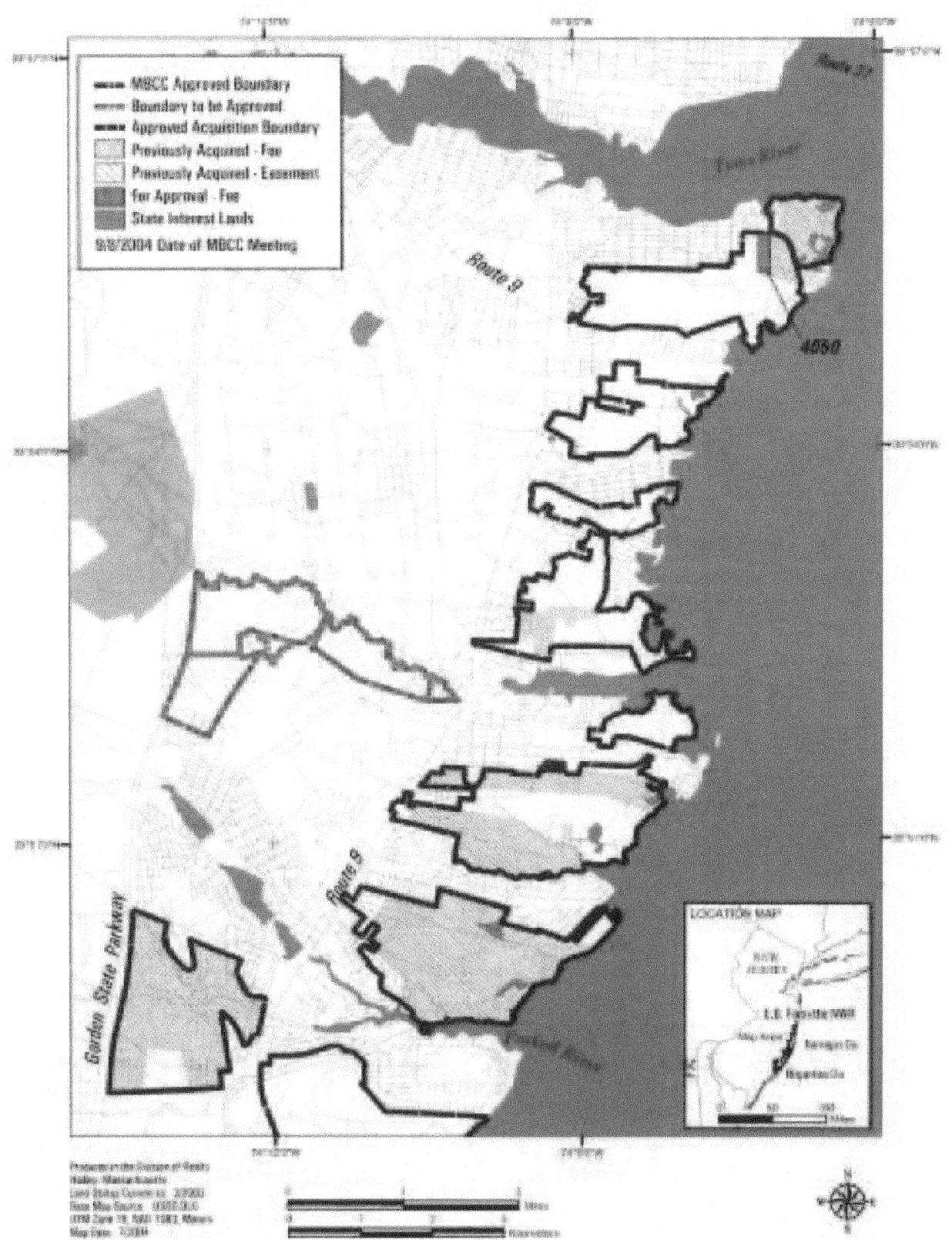

Lake Umbagog National Wildlife Refuge
Oxford County, Maine

CThe Lake Umbagog National Wildlife Refuge project area includes diverse and extensive palustrine, lacustrine, and riverine wetland complexes recognized as the some of the finest wildlife habitat in the states of New Hampshire and Maine. Located on the northern part of the New Hampshire/Maine border, the 23,184 acre project includes wetland habitat in both New Hampshire and Maine. Both states are setting aside additional lands to complement the protection of the Lake Umbagog watershed. Lake Umbagog has been listed by both states as a priority site for acquisition under the Atlantic Coast Joint Venture of the North American Waterfowl Management Plan, as well as identified for protection under the Emergency Wetlands Resources Act of 1986. A portion of the project area has already been designated as the Floating Bog National Natural Landmark by the National Park Service.

Wildlife values include waterfowl production and migration habitat, with a large amount of forested wetland of particular importance to black ducks whose populations are declining, ring-necked ducks, and cavity nesters such as wood ducks, goldeneye, and hooded mergansers. The first bald eagle nest in New Hampshire since 1949 is located in the project area, and several federal Species of Management Concern and state-listed threatened/endangered species are dependent on the area. Lake Umbagog is the most productive breeding site for the common loon in New Hampshire and is recognized as one of the most important breeding areas in the northeastern United States for its high nesting success. Additionally, the area is noted for its high nesting density of osprey. Large populations of moose and black bear also add to the wilderness quality of the area.

The Commission also approved the 466 acre refuge boundary addition and price approval for a 1,073 acre tract on September 8, 2004.

Lake Umbagog National Wildlife Refuge
Oxford County, Maine

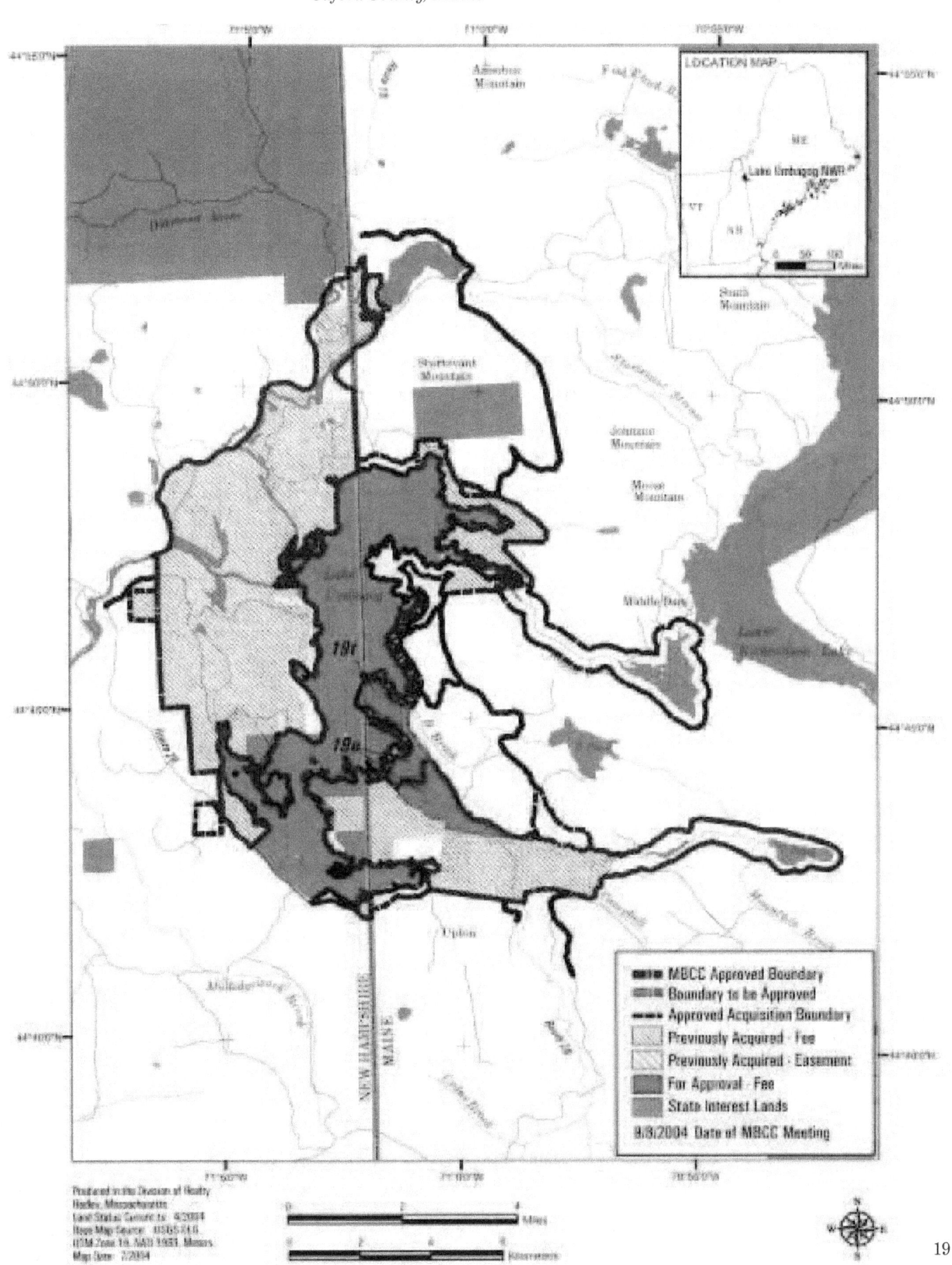

McFadden National Wildlife Refuge
Galveston County, Texas

On May 1, 1980, the Migratory Bird
Conservation Commission approved the
establishment of the McFaddin National
Wildlife Refuge, and the fee purchase of
41,682 acres at the Refuge using the
Migratory Bird Conservation Fund
(MBCC). Following these initial
approvals, the Commission approved the
acquisition of an additional 6,962 acres in
Fee and 7,748 by means of conservation
easement with MBCC. The last 212 acres
approved by the Commission February
25, 1997, never closed due to deaths in the
family etc. The total acreage of the
Refuge now stands at 56,180.

Acquisition of the proposed addition of
2,681 acres to McFaddin NWR, would
protect important wetland habitats for
migrating and wintering waterfowl.
Coastal marsh habitats on the property
provide feeding and resting areas for
waterfowl migrating through or wintering
on the upper Texas Coast. Twenty-three
species of ducks and four species of geese
have been observed on adjacent Refuge
lands. The marsh and neighboring
uplands provide excellent nesting and
brooding areas for the mottled duck, a
resident species of special concern due to
the recent population declines. This area
is within the North American Waterfowl
Management Plan's (NAWMP), Gulf
Coast Joint Venture-Chenier Plain
Initiative (GCJV-CPI) and is considered a
high priority for acquisition. It would
assist in meeting the habitat protection
goals of NAWMP and the GCJV-CPI, as
well as assist in sustaining waterfowl
populations at recommended levels and
maintaining their current distribution
across North America.

The Commission approved the refuge
boundary addition and price approval for
a 2,681 acre tract on June 9, 2004.

McFadden National Wildlife Refuge
Galveston County, Texas

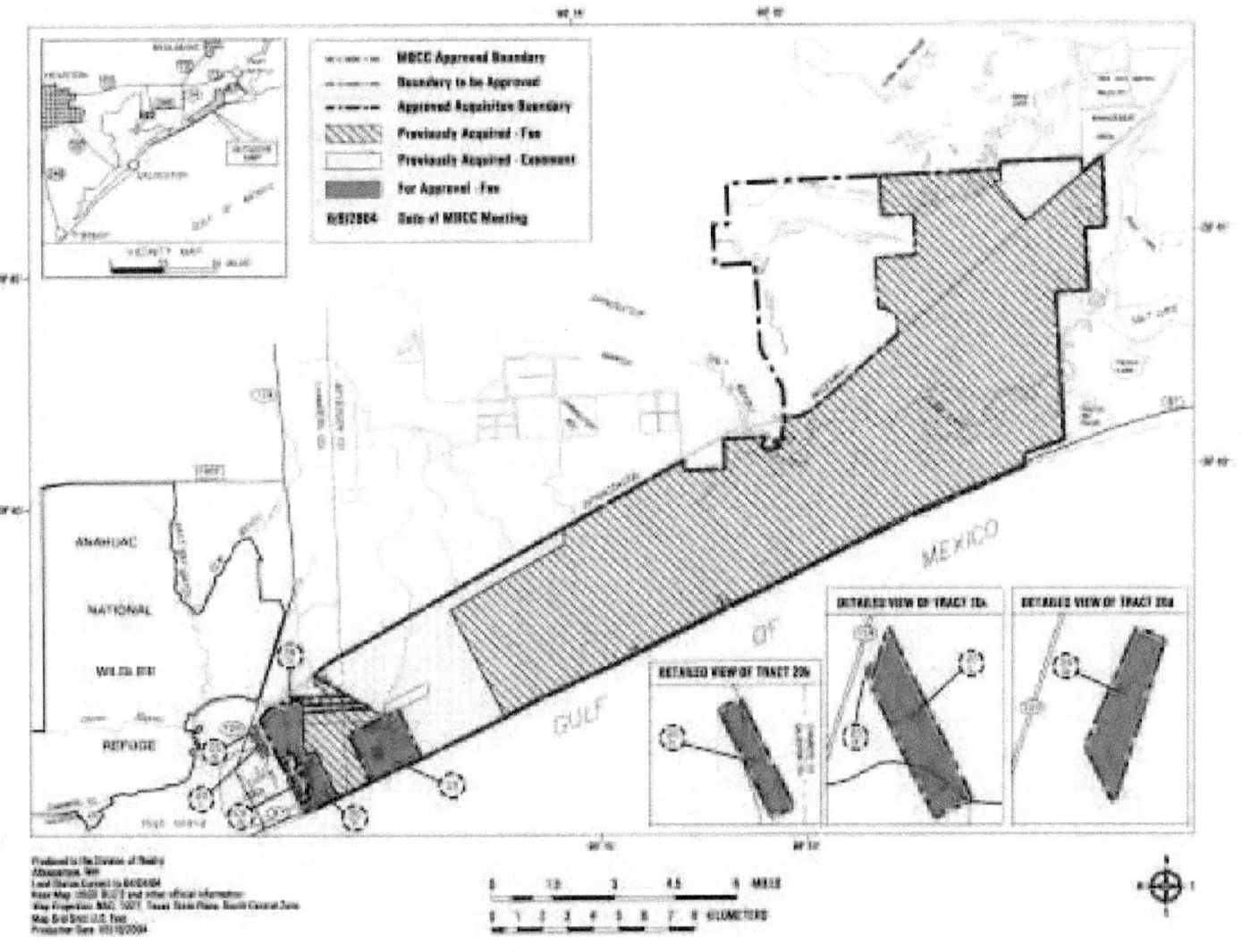

Rachel Carson National Wildlife Refuge
York and Cumberland Counties, Maine

Rachel Carson NWR was established to preserve ten estuaries along the Atlantic coast of Maine that provide important resting and wintering habitat to waterfowl and other migratory birds along with the Atlantic Flyway. Acquired lands total 5,187 acres in ten refuge divisions beginning at Kittery, Maine, northward along the coast communities to Cape Elizabeth, Maine.

A major emphasis at the refuge is salt marsh management. These salt marshes provide breeding habitat for black ducks and are especially important to wintering black ducks for foraging and shelter. During fall migration black ducks occur in modest numbers in salt marshes and bays throughout the refuge. During harsh winters, these marshes provide vital food and cover resources at a time when inland waters are frozen. The refuge also supports a breeding and summer resident population of waterfowl. Acquisition of this area will greatly increase the refuge's ability to provide important breeding and migration habitat for waterfowl, particularly black ducks, mallards and wood ducks as well as other migratory birds of concern to the USFWS. The goal of the refuge's restoration prescription for this area is to restore small ponds on the marsh surface so that aquatic life can survive and plug ditches to more closely mimic natural hydrology. The ponds provide habitat for submerged aquatic plants and aquatic insects. The Spartina salt marsh and dune grass along with several other natural communities form a coastal dune-salt marsh ecosystem in southern Maine.

The Commission approved the 275 acre refuge boundary addition and price approval for a 35 acre tract on September 8, 2004.

Rachel Carson National Wildlife Refuge
York and Cumberland Counties, Maine

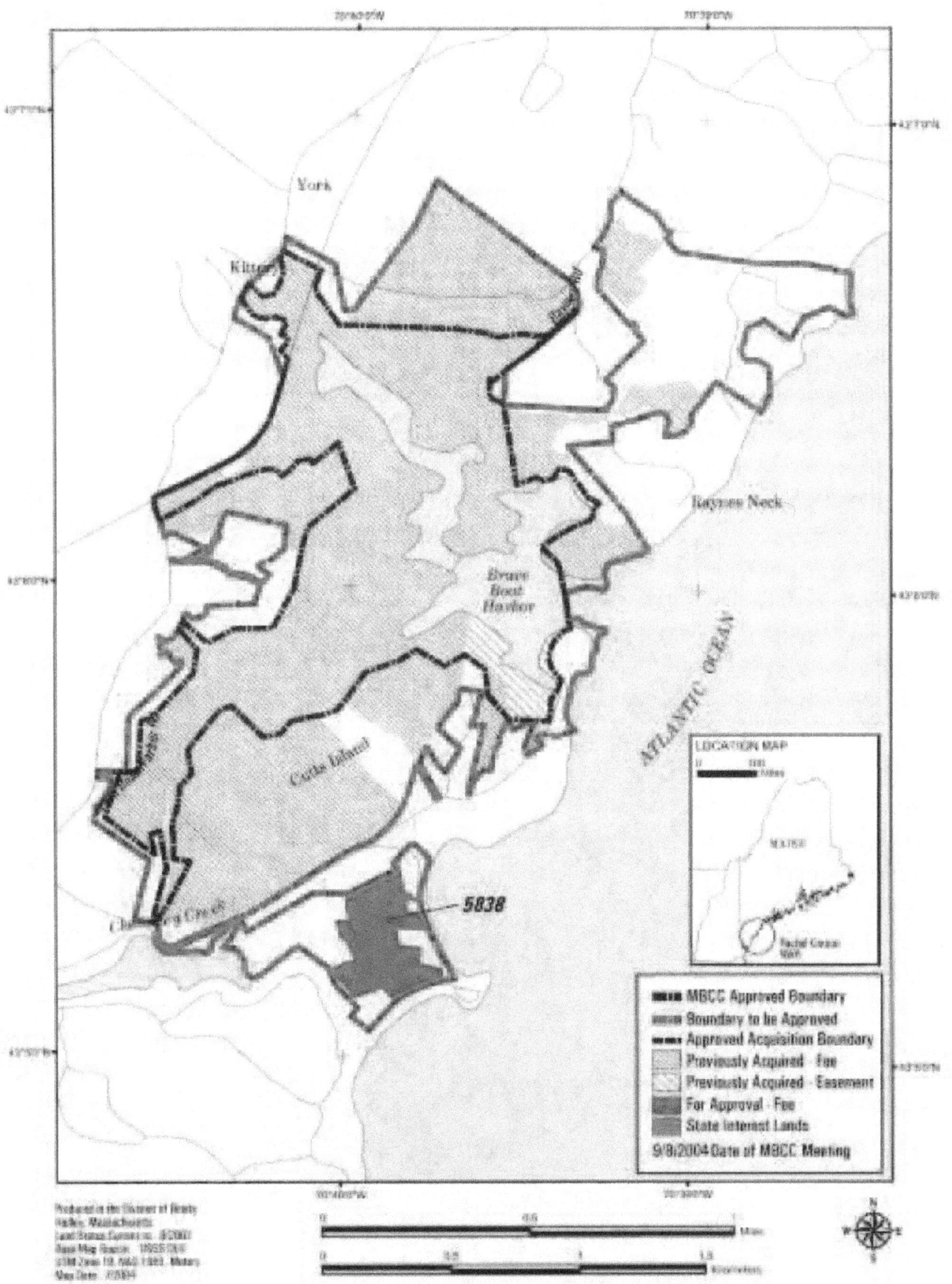

Red River National Wildlife Refuge
Caddo, Bossier, Desoto, Red River, and Natchitoches Parishes, Louisiana

Red River National Wildlife Refuge was established on October 13, 2000, under authority of the Red River National Wildlife Refuge Act (Public Law 106-300) to preserve, protect and restore 50,000 acres in five refuge units along a 280-mile stretch of the Red River in northwest Louisiana. To date, 4,532 acres have been acquired at this refuge with an additional 1,103 acres being leased.

The purposes of Red River NWR are to: restore and conserve native plants and animal communities in the Red River basin; provide habitat for migratory birds; and provide assistance to private landowners for the restoration of their lands for the benefit of fish and wildlife. This refuge provides wintering habitat for mallards, pintails and wood ducks, and contributes to the goals of the North American Waterfowl Management Plan. Reforestation and restoration of native habitats will benefit resident and migratory waterfowl as well a wide array of other species. In addition, the refuge offers recreational, research, and educational opportunities.

The Commission approved the 14,397 acre refuge boundary addition and price approval for a 1,082 acre tract on September 8, 2004.

Red River National Wildlife Refuge
Caddo, Bossier, Desoto, Red River, and Natchitoches Parishes, Louisiana

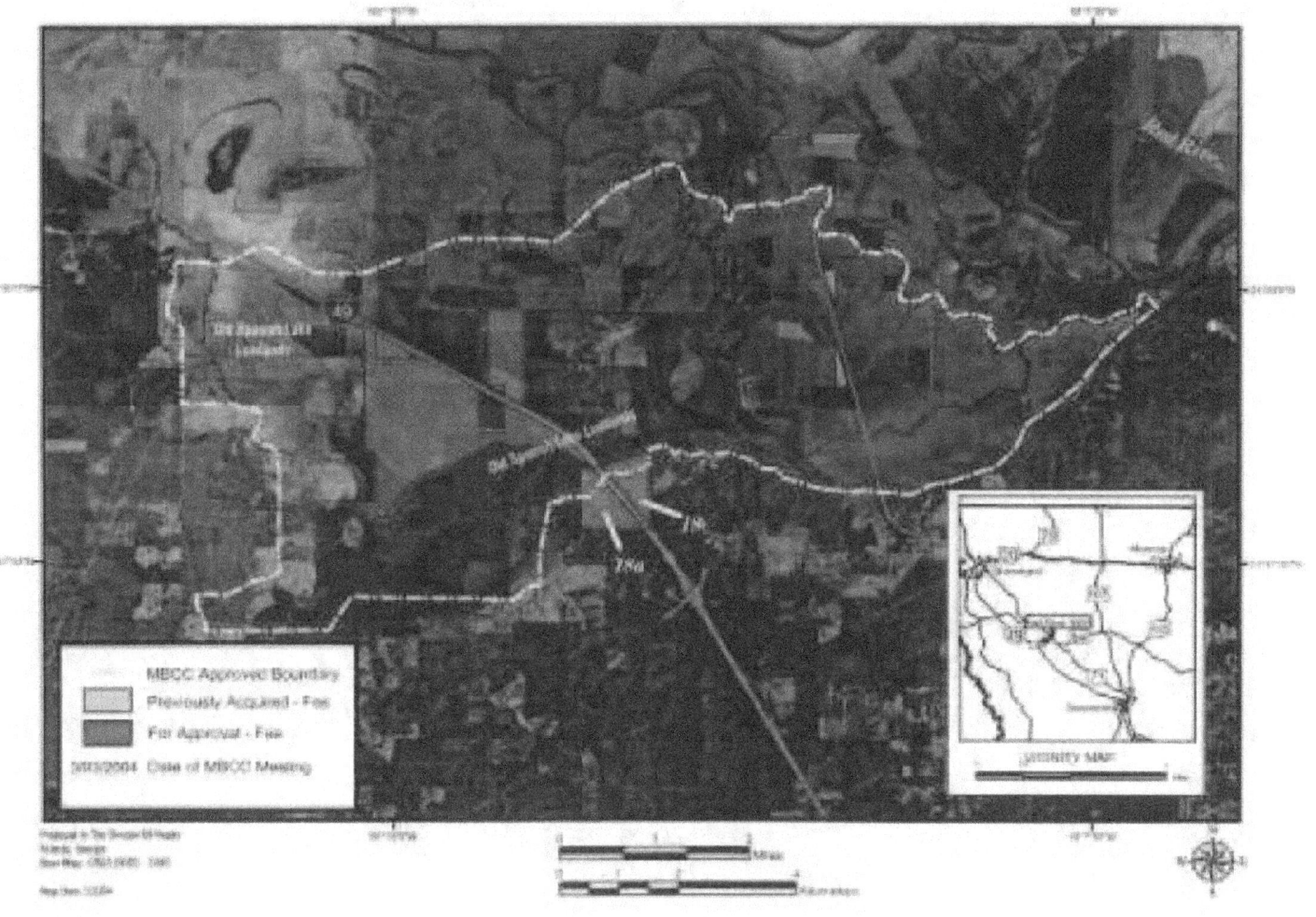

San Bernard National Wildlife Refuge
Brazoria and Fort Bend Counties, Texas

The San Bernard National Wildlife Refuge was approved by the Migratory Bird Conservation Commission on February 27,1968. To date, 36,698 acres have been acquired. In 1997, the Austin=s Woods Conservation Plan authorizing the acquisition of up to 28,000 acres of satellite units to San Bernard was approved. To date, 8,156 acres have been acquired through transfer from the Federal Deposit Insurance Corporation or through donations from various entities, or with funds approved by North American Wetlands Conservation Act, with funds obtained from mitigation, and by Migratory Bird Conservation Commission approval for the Austin's Woods Unit.

The proposed area is part of a productive and valuable wetland complex providing wintering, migration, and resident habitat for waterfowl, wading birds, neotropical migratory birds, and other wetland-dependent wildlife species. Thousands of waterfowl winter in the area. Mottled ducks, a species of concern, use the area, as well as green-winged teal, gadwalls, and black-bellied whistling ducks. This proposed acquisition is within the Mid-Coast Initiative of the Gulf Coast Joint Venture of the North American Waterfowl Management Plan.

The Commission approved the refuge boundary addition and price approval for a 1,681 acre tract on September 8, 2004.

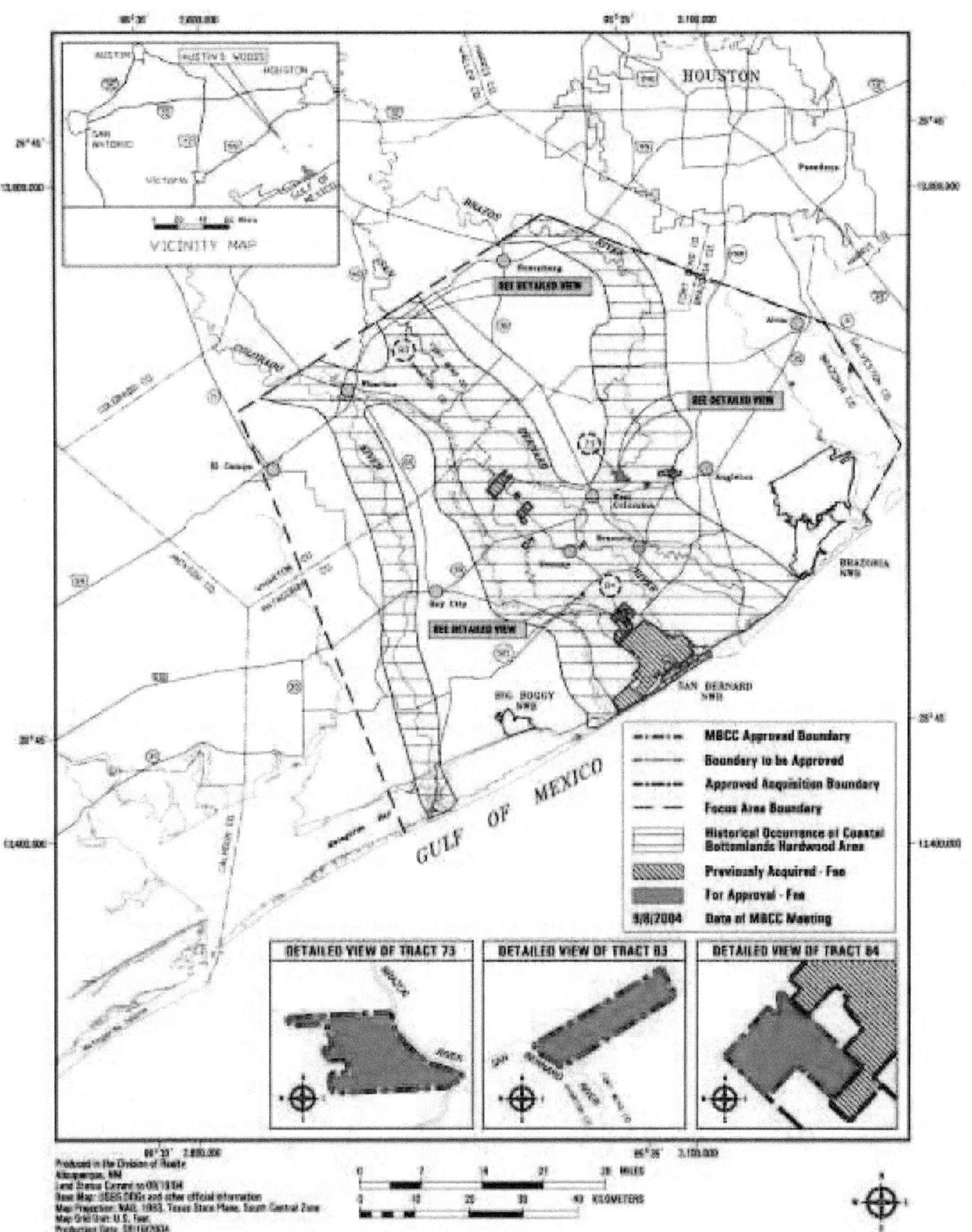

Silvio O. Conte National Wildlife Refuge
Coos County, New Hampshire

The Silvio O. Conte National Fish and Wildlife Refuge (Refuge) was launched with the introduction of legislation by the late Congressman Silvio O. Conte which authorized a national fish and wildlife refuge within the Connecticut River watershed. Congressman Conte was a member of Congress for over 30 years and served on the Migratory Bird Conservation Commission for about 27 years. After his death, Congress renamed the refuge the Silvio O. Conte National Fish and Wildlife Refuge.

The Final Environmental Impact Statement (FEIS) for the Silvio O. Conte Refuge was completed and a Record of Decision authorizing the Refuge was signed by the Regional Director on December 13, 1995. Within the 7.2 million acre Connecticut River watershed, 65 Special Focus Areas important for resource protection were identified in Connecticut, Massachusetts, New Hampshire, and Vermont. The Refuge was officially established on October 3, 1997 with the acquisition of the 3.8 acre Third Island, located in the Connecticut River in Deerfield, Massachusetts. Approximately 30,430 acres of the proposed 91,500 acres have been acquired to date. The Pondicherry Division was established with the purchase of three tracts (670 acres) from one land owner on December 22, 2000.

The Commission approved the 5,103 acre refuge boundary addition and price approval for a 622 acre tract on September 8, 2004.

Silvio O. Conte National Wildlife Refuge
Coos County, New Hampshire

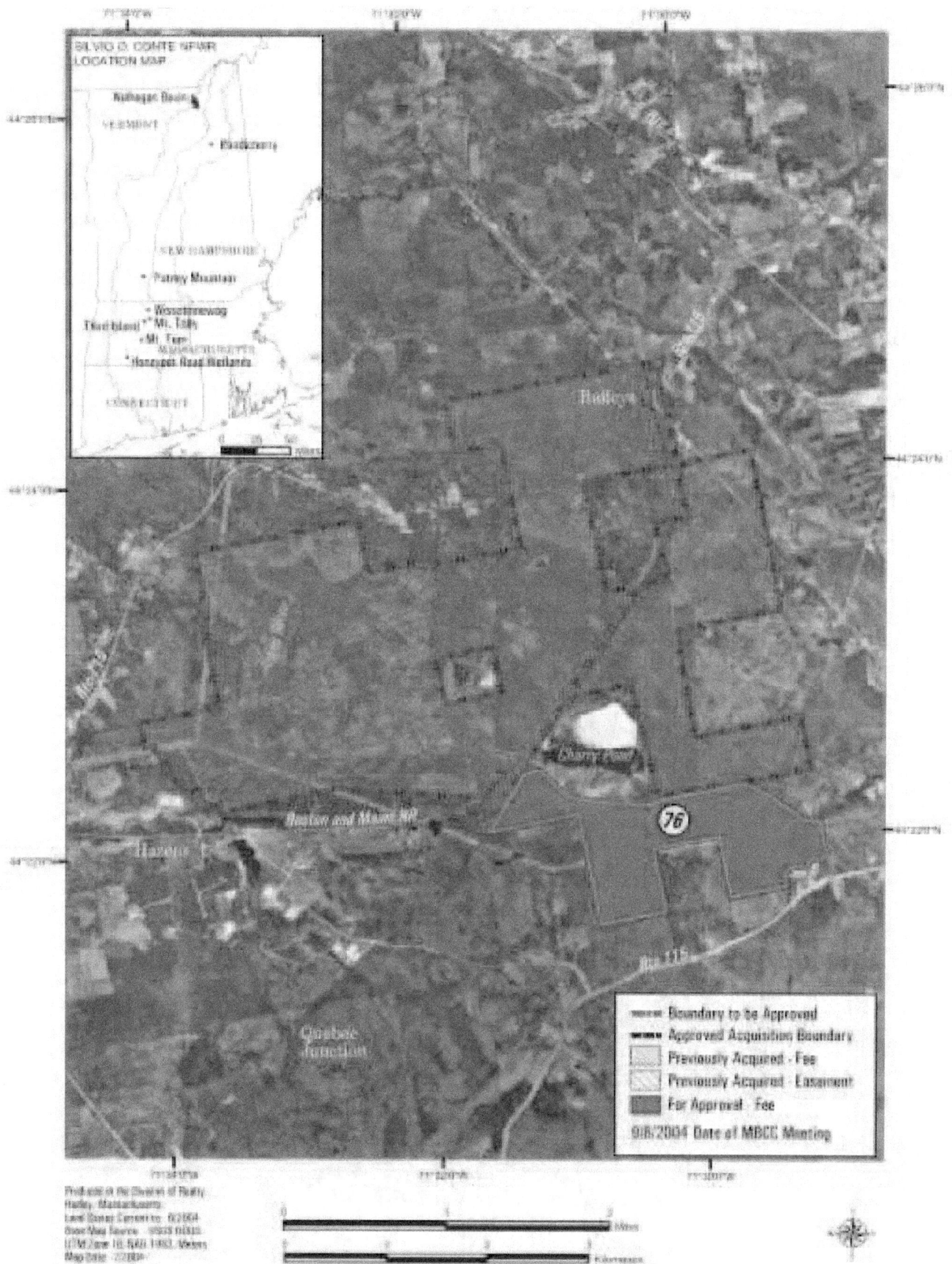

Trinity River National Wildlife Refuge
Liberty County, Texas

The Trinity River National Wildlife Refuge (Refuge) was established on January 3, 1994, with the purchase of 4,400 acres of bottomland hardwood and associated habitats in Liberty County, Texas. These lands were purchased with Land and Water Conservation Fund dollars totaling $3,270,000. Since 1994, an additional 4,195 acres have been purchased with LWCF dollars totaling $1,941,500. On June 14, 1994, the Migratory Bird Conservation Commission approved the initial MBCC boundary for the Refuge, encompassing 19,220 acres. Since 1994, the MBCC boundary has been expanded by the Service to include another 10,498 acres. To date, 9,617 acres have been purchased with Migratory Bird Conservation Funds totaling $5,974,172.

The Trinity River NWR protects remnant bottomland hardwood and associated wetland habitats for migrating, wintering and breeding waterfowl. Additionally, it represents one of the few remaining high quality areas for waterfowl in East Texas. It provides essential foraging and/or roosting habitat for the wood duck, mallard, gadwall, widgeon, green and blue-winged teal, lesser scaup and mottled duck. Mature cavity trees dispersed throughout the area provide important nesting habitat for wood ducks and black-bellied whistling ducks. Numerous colonial waterbird rookeries are found in swamps throughout the project area.

The Commission approved the refuge boundary addition and price approval for a 255 acre tract on September 8, 2004.

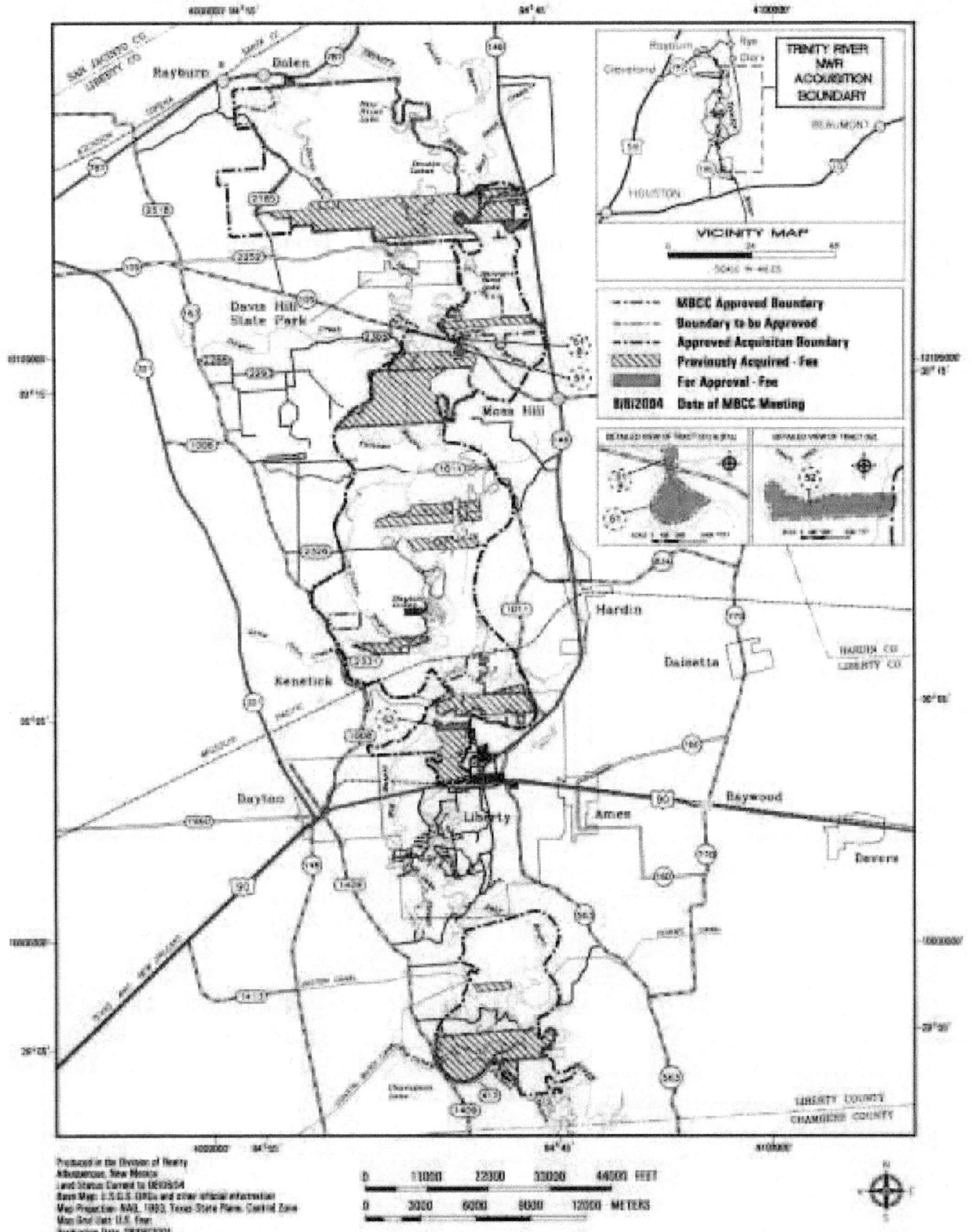

Membership of the National Migratory Bird Conservation Commission

Fiscal Year	Secretary of the Interior[1]	Secretary of Agriculture[2]	Secretary of Commerce[3]	Secretary of Transportation[4]	Administrator of Environmental Protection Agency[5]	Members on Part of the Senate		Members on Part of the House		Secretary to the Commission
1929	Roy L. Wilbur	Arthur M. Hyde	Robert P. Lamont			Harry B. Hawes	Peter Norbeck	Sam D. McReynolds	Ernest R. Ackerman	Rudolph Dieffenbach
1930										
1931										
1932									August H. Anderson	
1933	Harold L. Ickes	Henry A. Wallace	Daniel C. Roper			Key Pittman			Roy O. Woodruff	
1934									Chester C. Bolton	
1935										
1936										
1937							Charles L. McNary		James Wolfenden	
1938										
1939			Harry L. Hopkins							
1940		Claude R. Wickard						John J. Cochran		
1941			Jessie H. Jones			George L. Radcliffe				
1942										
1943										
1944							Vacant			
1945	Julius A. Krug	Clinton P. Anderson	Henry A. Wallace				C. Wayland Brooks		Walter E. Brehm	
1946						A. Willis Robertson		Frank M. Karsten		
1947			W. Averell Harriman							
1948		Charles F. Brannon	Charles W. Sawyer							Arthur A. Riemer
1949							Raymond E. Baldwin			
1950	Oscar L. Chapman						Vacant			
1951							John W. Bricker		August H. Anderson	
1952										
1953	Douglas McKay	Ezra Taft Benson	Sinclair Weeks							
1954										
1955						Thomas C. Hennings, Jr.				
1956	Fred A. Seaton									
1957										Albert J. Rissman
1958										
1959			Lewis L. Strauss				Roman L. Hruska		Leon H. Gavin	
1960			Frederick H. Mueller							
1961	Stewart L. Udall	Orville L. Freeman	Luther H. Hodges			Lee Metcalf				
1962										
1963										
1964									George A. Gooding	
1965			John T. Connor						Silvio O. Conte	F.G. Spoden Jr.
1966										
1967			Alexander B. Trowbridge	Alan S. Boyd						
1968										
1969	Walter J. Hickel	Clifford M. Hardin		John A. Volpe		Joseph D. Tydings	Henry L. Bellman	John D. Dingell		
1970	Roger C.B. Morton					Lee Metcalf				Walter R. McAllester
1971		Earl L. Butz								
1972										
1973				Claude S. Brinegar						
1974										
1975	Stanley Hathaway			William T. Coleman		Quentin N. Burdick				
1976	Thomas S. Kleppe	Bob Bergland								
1977	Cecil D. Andrus			Brook Adams		Floyd K. Haskell				
1978										
1979				Neil Golldschmidt		David H. Pryor				
1980										
1981	James G. Watt	James R. Block		Drew Lewis			Thad Cochran			
1982										
1983	William P. Clark			Elizabeth H. Dole						
1984	Donald Hodel									
1985		Richard Lyng								
1986										William F. Hartwig
1987										
1988				James Burnley IV						
1989	Manuel Lujan Jr.	Clayton Yeutter		Samuel K. Skinner	William K. Reilly					
1990										
1991		Edward R. Madigan								
1992									Richard T. Schulze	
1993	Bruce Babbit	Mike Espy			Carol M. Browner					Geoffrey L. Haskett
1994										
1995		Daniel R. Glickman				John B. Breaux			Curt Weldon	
1996										Jeffrey M. Donahoe
1997										
1998										
1999										
2000										
2001	Gale Norton	Ann M. Veneman			Christine Todd-Whitman					
2002										
2003					Michael O. Leavitt					A. Eric Alvarez

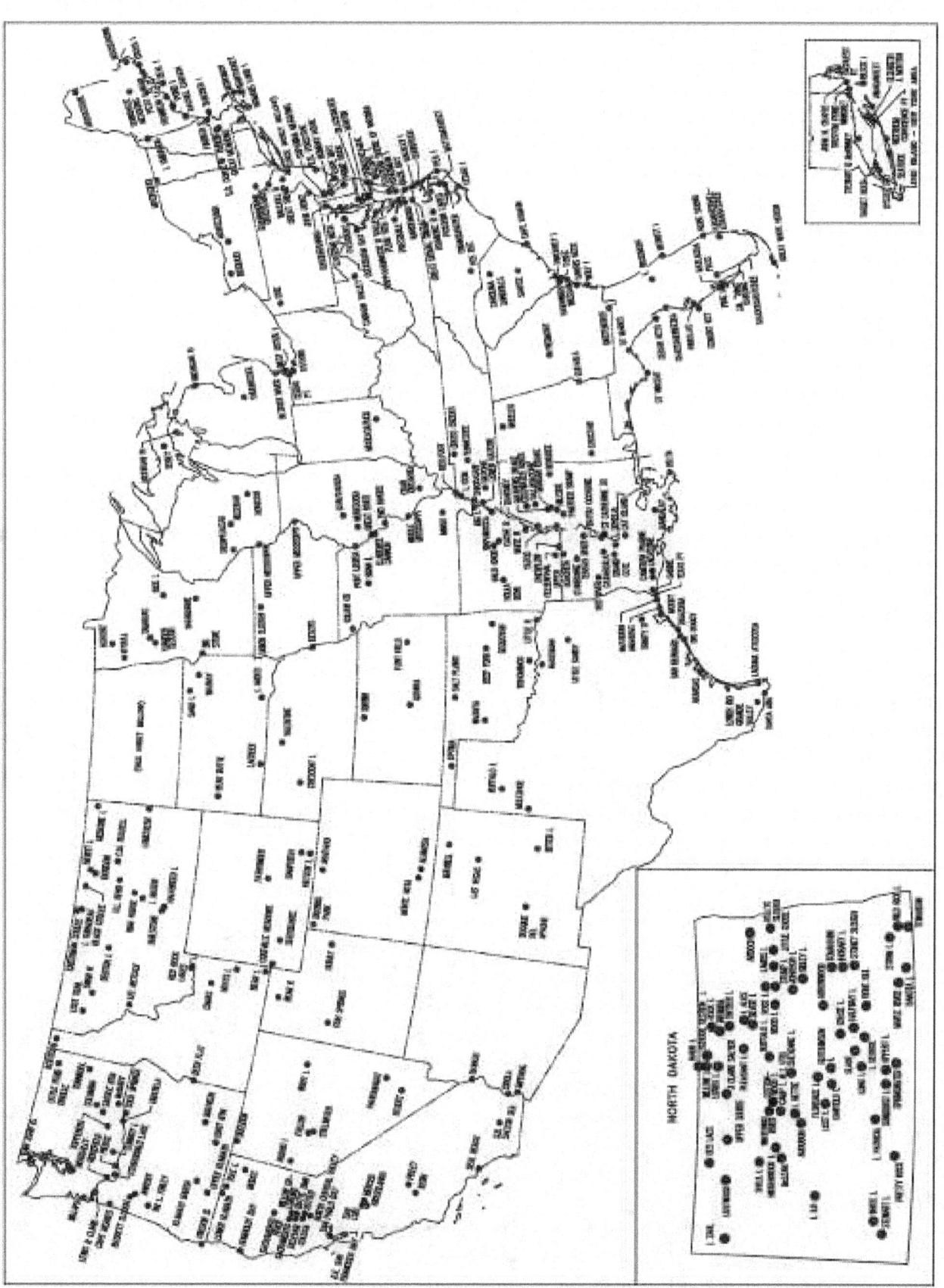

Migratory Bird Conservation Commission
National Migratory Bird Refuge Areas

COMPILED IN THE DIVISION OF REALTY
WASHINGTON, DC   SEPTEMBER 30, 2004

Wetland Management Districts of the National Wildlife Refuge System

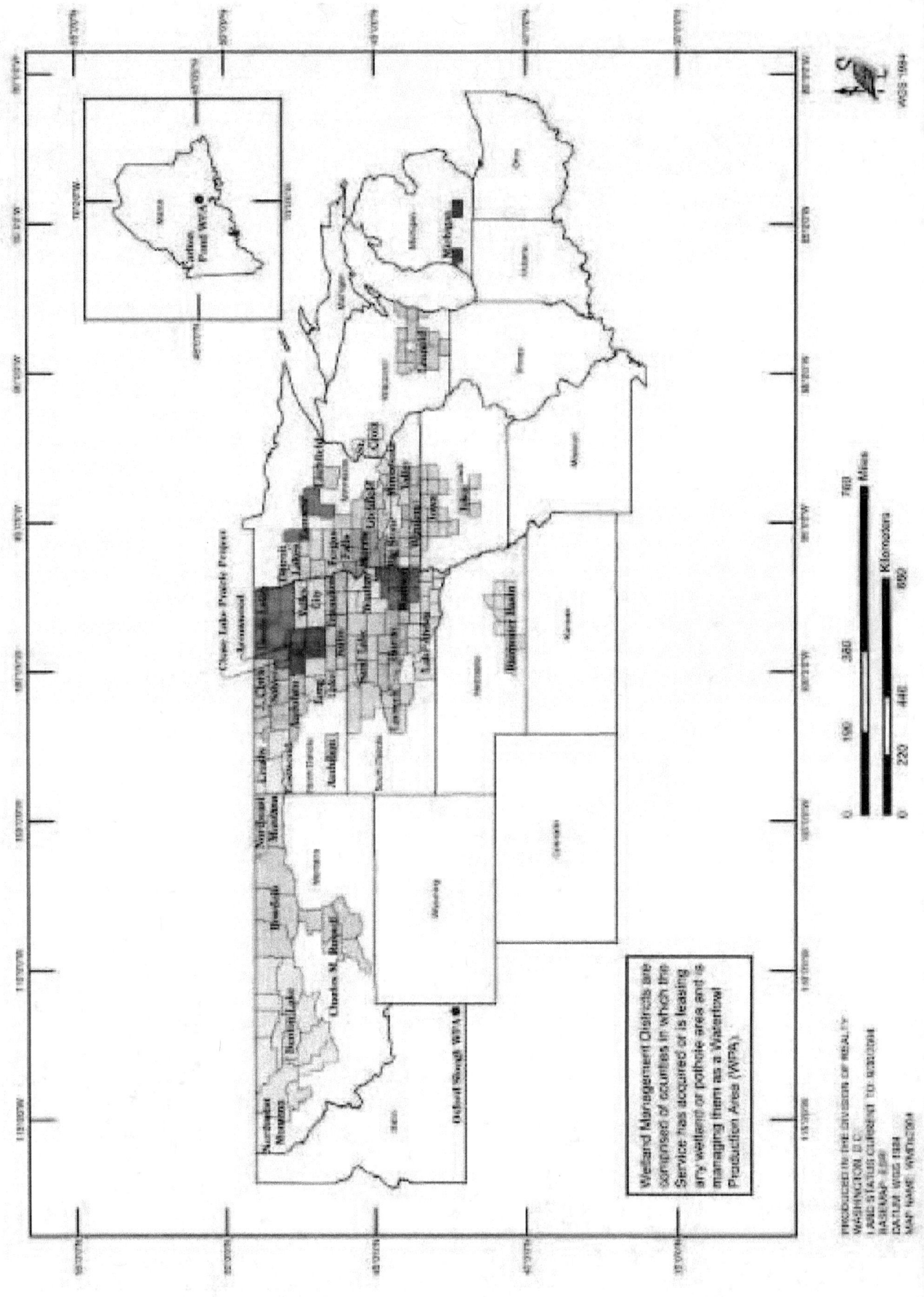

Notes on Tables One and Two

The information contained in this report includes those acquisitions and dispositions of land and interests therein that are purchased with Migratory Bird Conservation Fund monies or acquired under the authority of the Migratory Bird Conservation Act. It also includes other migratory bird areas such as those that are transferred to the Fish and Wildlife Service under the authority of Public Law 80-537 to carry out a migratory bird management program (these will appear on Table 1).

In an ongoing effort to improve data quality, the figures in Tables One and Two may show minor changes from previous annual reports. Lands in which the Service previously acquired a less-than-fee interest (leases and easements) may be purchased in fee during the year, and the number of easement or lease acres will show a decrease and the number of purchased acres an increase. The acreage appearing in the Approvals and Summary of Land Acquisitions sections of this report will not appear in Tables One or Two until after the tracts are acquired and the funds are actually expended. Also, a newly approved refuge will not appear on Table One until the tracts are acquired.

For information on all lands and interests under U.S. Fish and Wildlife Service control, refer to the "Annual Report of Lands Under Control of the U.S. Fish and Wildlife Service." This report can be obtained from the U.S. Fish and Wildlife Service Division of Realty at http://realty.fws.gov or by calling (703) 358-1713.

TABLE 1 - NATIONAL MIGRATORY BIRDS AREAS IN THE CONTERMINOUS UNITED STATES

State and Unit	FISCAL YEAR MBCF ACQUISITION				CUMULATIVE TOTALS AT END OF FISCAL YEAR					
	Purchased		Easement or Lease		MBCF				All Other	Total
					Purchased		Easement or Lease			
	Acres	Cost	Acres	Cost	Acres	Cost	Acres	Cost	Acres	Acres
ALABAMA										
CHOCTAW	0.00	0.00	0.00	0.00	0.00	0.00	0.00	0.00	4,218.00	4,218.00
EUFAULA (1)	0.00	0.00	0.00	0.00	0.00	0.00	0.00	0.00	7,953.19	7,953.19
FSA INTEREST AL** *	0.00	0.00	0.00	0.00	0.00	0.00	0.00	0.00	742.69	742.69
WHEELER	0.00	0.00	0.00	0.00	50.70	0.00	0.00	0.00	34,379.96	34,430.66
TOTAL 3	0.00	0.00	0.00	0.00	50.70	0.00	0.00	0.00	47,293.84	47,344.54
ARIZONA										
CIBOLA (2)	0.00	0.00	0.00	0.00	0.00	0.00	0.00	0.00	8,606.04	8,606.04
HAVASU (2)	0.00	0.00	0.00	0.00	0.00	0.00	0.00	0.00	30,279.82	30,279.82
IMPERIAL (2)	0.00	0.00	0.00	0.00	0.00	0.00	0.00	0.00	17,809.76	17,809.76
TOTAL 3	0.00	0.00	0.00	0.00	0.00	0.00	0.00	0.00	56,695.62	56,695.62
ARKANSAS										
BALD KNOB	0.00	0.00	0.00	0.00	4,536.00	3,002,000.00	0.00	0.00	10,273.95	14,809.95
BIG LAKE	0.00	0.00	0.00	0.00	562.91	31,854.69	.25	2.00	10,472.94	11,036.10
CACHE RIVER	1,158.00	2,000,000.00	0.00	0.00	43,816.63	38,057,435.92	0.00	0.00	17,121.68	60,938.31
FELSENTHAL	0.00	0.00	0.00	0.00	0.00	0.00	0.00	0.00	64,902.14	64,902.14
FSA INTEREST AR** *	0.00	0.00	0.00	0.00	0.00	0.00	0.00	0.00	3,458.67	3,458.67
HOLLA BEND	0.00	0.00	0.00	0.00	690.45	336,903.00	0.00	5,175.00	5,608.58	6,299.03
OVERFLOW	0.00	0.00	0.00	0.00	13,042.89	10,407,020.50	0.00	0.00	0.00	13,042.89
WAPANOCCA	0.00	0.00	0.00	0.00	5,484.17	1,351,416.00	0.00	0.00	0.00	5,484.17
WHITE RIVER	0.00	0.00	0.00	0.00	10,145.63	5,254,645.37	413.22	22.00	147,855.87	158,414.72
TOTAL 8	1,158.00	2,000,000.00	0.00	0.00	78,278.68	58,441,275.48	413.47	5,199.00	259,693.83	338,385.98
CALIFORNIA										
BUTTE SINK	0.00	0.00	0.00	0.00	514.98	1,650,700.00	10,310.64	12,816,903.00	217.88	11,043.50
CIBOLA (3) *	0.00	0.00	0.00	0.00	0.00	0.00	0.00	0.00	4,246.52	4,246.52
COLUSA	0.00	0.00	0.00	0.00	2,384.74	107,313.30	0.00	0.00	1,655.24	4,039.98
DELEVAN	0.00	0.00	0.00	0.00	5,796.54	2,345,739.00	0.00	175,000.00	0.00	5,796.54
DON EDWARDS SAN FRAN. BAY	0.00	0.00	0.00	0.00	0.00	0.00	0.00	0.00	29,972.89	29,972.89
FSA INTEREST CA** *	0.00	0.00	0.00	0.00	0.00	0.00	0.00	0.00	80.00	80.00
GRASSLANDS	1,905.40	4,255,000.00	1,093.50	1,202,850.00	6,442.28	9,158,896.00	68,753.47	32,066,291.00	8,527.97	83,723.72
HAVASU (3) *	0.00	0.00	0.00	0.00	0.00	0.00	0.00	0.00	7,235.34	7,235.34
HUMBOLDT BAY	264.20	125,000.00	0.00	0.00	2,717.60	5,254,410.00	0.00	0.00	488.32	3,205.92
IMPERIAL (3) *	0.00	0.00	0.00	0.00	0.00	0.00	0.00	0.00	7,958.19	7,958.19
KERN	0.00	0.00	0.00	0.00	10,543.86	579,912.00	0.00	0.00	705.31	11,249.17
LOWER KLAMATH (4)	0.00	0.00	0.00	0.00	4,530.53	3,390,123.00	0.00	0.00	39,763.61	44,294.14
MERCED	0.00	0.00	0.00	0.00	3,803.82	2,180,000.00	0.00	0.00	1.76	3,805.58
MODOC	0.00	0.00	0.00	0.00	5,359.58	1,077,634.19	0.00	0.00	1,661.65	7,021.23
NORTH CENTRAL VALLEY	0.00	0.00	593.95	1,098,808.00	586.63	1,565,531.00	7,093.19	10,600,898.00	7,239.72	14,919.54
PIXLEY	0.00	0.00	0.00	0.00	0.00	0.00	0.00	0.00	6,389.13	6,389.13
SACRAMENTO	0.00	0.00	0.00	0.00	10,775.61	150,498.00	0.00	0.00	43.39	10,819.00
SACRAMENTO RIVER	0.00	0.00	0.00	0.00	126.40	145,000.00	0.00	0.00	10,521.65	10,648.05
SAN JOAQUIN RIVER	0.00	0.00	0.00	0.00	1,239.18	7,030,819.00	0.00	0.00	8,484.28	9,723.46
SAN LUIS	0.00	0.00	0.00	0.00	7,422.41	2,171,055.00	703.00	2,284,000.00	14,768.00	22,893.41
SAN PABLO BAY	0.00	0.00	0.00	0.00	248.00	243,400.00	0.00	0.00	12,941.72	13,189.72
SEAL BEACH	0.00	0.00	0.00	0.00	0.00	0.00	0.00	0.00	910.71	910.71
SONNY BONO SALTON SEA	0.00	0.00	0.00	0.00	9,342.14	294,461.80	637.00	1,089.27	27,679.73	37,658.87
SUTTER	0.00	0.00	0.00	0.00	2,590.16	291,281.80	0.00	3,850.00	0.00	2,590.16
TULE LAKE	0.00	0.00	0.00	0.00	0.00	0.00	0.00	0.00	39,116.58	39,116.58
WILLOW CREEK-LURLINE	0.00	0.00	0.00	0.00	0.00	0.00	5,467.50	6,686,633.00	0.00	5,467.50
TOTAL 22	2,169.60	4,380,000.00	1,687.45	2,301,658.00	74,424.46	37,636,774.09	92,964.80	64,634,664.27	230,609.59	397,998.85
COLORADO										
ALAMOSA	0.00	0.00	0.00	0.00	10,904.78	2,377,463.16	0.00	24,035.90	1,121.59	12,026.37
ARAPAHO	0.00	0.00	0.00	0.00	17,771.88	4,798,286.00	0.00	35,358.66	5,497.64	23,269.52
BROWNS PARK	0.00	0.00	0.00	1,690.70	5,275.63	614,976.00	1,305.42	66,428.06	6,874.25	13,455.30
FSA INTEREST CO * * *	0.00	0.00	0.00	0.00	0.00	0.00	0.00	0.00	338.64	338.64
MONTE VISTA	0.00	0.00	0.00	0.00	13,950.66	2,241,750.00	0.00	0.00	883.33	14,833.99
TOTAL 4	0.00	0.00	0.00	1,690.70	47,902.95	10,032,475.16	1,305.42	125,822.62	14,715.45	63,923.82
CONNECTICUT										
STEWART B. MCKINNEY	0.00	0.00	0.00	0.00	361.24	2,263,560.00	0.00	0.00	547.57	908.81
TOTAL 1	0.00	0.00	0.00	0.00	361.24	2,263,560.00	0.00	0.00	547.57	908.81

TABLE 1 - NATIONAL MIGRATORY BIRDS AREAS IN THE CONTERMINOUS UNITED STATES (continued)

	FISCAL YEAR MBCF ACQUISITION				CUMULATIVE TOTALS AT END OF FISCAL YEAR					
					MBCF					
	Purchased		Easement or Lease		Purchased		Easement or Lease		All Other	Total
State and Unit	Acres	Cost	Acres	Cost	Acres	Cost	Acres	Cost	Acres	Acres
DELAWARE										
BOMBAY HOOK	0.00	0.00	0.00	0.00	15,256.81	1,619,288.60	0.00	2.00	800.95	16,057.76
FSA INTEREST DE ***	0.00	0.00	0.00	0.00	0.00	0.00	0.00	0.00	2.60	2.60
PRIME HOOK	0.00	0.00	0.00	0.00	8,276.67	3,620,268.16	79.19	5,346.20	1,757.25	10,113.11
TOTAL 2	0.00	0.00	0.00	0.00	23,533.48	5,239,556.76	79.19	5,346.20	2,560.80	26,173.47
FLORIDA										
ARTHUR R. MARSHALL	0.00	0.00	0.00	0.00	2,549.77	118,511.97	0.00	0.00	141,404.00	143,953.77
CALOOSAHATCHEE	0.00	0.00	0.00	0.00	0.00	0.00	0.00	0.00	40.00	40.00
CEDAR KEYS	0.00	0.00	0.00	0.00	0.00	0.00	0.00	0.00	891.15	891.15
CHASSAHOWITZKA	0.00	0.00	0.00	0.00	22,556.82	267,529.26	0.00	0.00	8,286.09	30,842.91
EGMONT KEY	0.00	0.00	0.00	0.00	0.00	0.00	0.00	0.00	328.30	328.30
FSA INTEREST FL ***	0.00	0.00	0.00	0.00	0.00	0.00	0.00	0.00	2,977.33	2,977.33
GREAT WHITE HERON	0.00	0.00	0.00	0.00	1,326.54	906,195.00	0.00	0.00	116,356.59	117,683.13
HOBE SOUND	0.00	0.00	0.00	0.00	0.00	0.00	0.00	0.00	1,034.98	1,034.98
J. N. DING DARLING	0.00	0.00	0.00	0.00	541.98	372,370.00	0.00	0.00	5,848.70	6,390.68
LAKE WOODRUFF	0.00	0.00	0.00	0.00	18,413.39	1,340,310.75	0.00	0.00	3,145.63	21,559.02
MATLACHA PASS	0.00	0.00	0.00	0.00	0.00	0.00	0.00	0.00	538.25	538.25
MERRITT ISLAND	0.00	0.00	0.00	0.00	0.00	0.00	0.00	0.00	139,189.40	139,189.40
OKEFENOKEE (1)	0.00	0.00	0.00	0.00	0.00	0.00	0.00	0.00	3,724.48	3,724.48
PINE ISLAND	0.00	0.00	0.00	0.00	0.00	0.00	0.00	0.00	602.24	602.24
PINELLAS	0.00	0.00	0.00	0.00	0.00	0.00	0.00	0.00	394.35	394.35
ST. MARKS	0.00	0.00	0.00	0.00	30,985.17	102,311.61	116.72	0.00	37,871.30	68,973.19
ST. VINCENT	0.00	0.00	0.00	0.00	12,358.20	2,035,000.00	0.00	0.00	131.73	12,489.93
TOTAL 16	0.00	0.00	0.00	0.00	88,731.87	5,142,228.59	116.72	0.00	538,089.47	626,938.06
GEORGIA										
EUFAULA (5) *	0.00	0.00	0.00	0.00	0.00	0.00	0.00	0.00	3,231.00	3,231.00
FSA INTEREST GA ***	0.00	0.00	0.00	0.00	0.00	0.00	0.00	0.00	4,795.57	4,795.57
HARRIS NECK	0.00	0.00	0.00	0.00	0.00	0.00	0.00	0.00	2,823.92	2,823.92
OKEFENOKEE (6) *	0.00	0.00	0.00	0.00	345,208.94	867,318.12	0.00	0.00	46,193.05	391,401.99
PIEDMONT	0.00	0.00	0.00	0.00	473.97	44,000.00	0.00	0.00	34,493.01	34,966.98
SAVANNAH (7)	0.00	0.00	0.00	0.00	8,027.84	1,705,352.40	0.00	0.00	5,295.64	13,323.48
WASSAW	0.00	0.00	0.00	0.00	0.00	0.00	0.00	0.00	10,069.87	10,069.87
WOLF ISLAND	0.00	0.00	0.00	0.00	4,587.82	120,813.52	0.00	0.00	538.00	5,125.82
TOTAL 5	0.00	0.00	0.00	0.00	358,298.57	2,737,484.04	0.00	0.00	107,440.06	465,738.63
IDAHO										
BEAR LAKE	0.00	0.00	0.00	0.00	626.57	212,279.30	0.00	1.00	17,459.01	18,085.58
CAMAS	0.00	0.00	0.00	0.00	10,438.46	202,700.84	0.00	0.00	139.88	10,578.34
DEER FLAT (4)	0.00	0.00	0.00	0.00	242.89	26,415.50	0.00	0.00	10,304.68	10,547.57
FSA INTEREST ID***	0.00	0.00	0.00	0.00	0.00	0.00	0.00	0.00	1,110.60	1,110.60
GRAYS LAKE	0.00	0.00	0.00	0.00	4,069.78	1,843,000.00	32.49	4,518.30	16,022.81	20,125.08
KOOTENAI	0.00	0.00	0.00	0.00	2,774.15	708,100.00	0.00	0.00	0.14	2,774.29
TOTAL 5	0.00	0.00	0.00	0.00	18,151.85	2,992,495.64	32.49	4,519.30	45,037.12	63,221.46
ILLINOIS										
CHAUTAUQUA	0.00	0.00	0.00	0.00	44.54	2,525.38	0.00	0.00	6,401.03	6,445.57
CRAB ORCHARD	0.00	0.00	0.00	0.00	216.40	390,416.00	0.00	0.00	43,661.74	43,878.14
FSA INTEREST IL ***	0.00	0.00	0.00	0.00	0.00	0.00	0.00	0.00	335.40	335.40
GREAT RIVER (8)	0.00	0.00	0.00	0.00	1,559.87	353,202.72	0.00	0.00	5,550.76	7,110.63
MEREDOSIA	0.00	0.00	0.00	0.00	0.00	0.00	0.00	0.00	3,400.80	3,400.80
MIDDLE MISSISSIPPI RIVER	0.00	0.00	0.00	0.00	0.00	0.00	0.00	0.00	2,237.53	2,237.53
PORT LOUISA (19)	0.00	0.00	0.00	0.00	0.00	0.00	0.00	0.00	1,470.89	1,470.89
TWO RIVERS (8)	0.00	0.00	0.00	0.00	796.17	346,943.00	0.00	0.00	7,237.03	8,033.20
TOTAL 7	0.00	0.00	0.00	0.00	2,616.98	1,093,087.10	0.00	0.00	70,295.18	72,912.16
INDIANA										
FSA INTEREST IN ***	0.00	0.00	0.00	0.00	0.00	0.00	0.00	0.00	219.03	219.03
MUSCATATUCK	0.00	0.00	0.00	0.00	7,713.53	3,582,787.72	0.00	0.00	88.69	7,802.22
TOTAL 1	0.00	0.00	0.00	0.00	7,713.53	3,582,787.72	0.00	0.00	307.72	8,021.25
IOWA										
DESOTO (10)	0.00	0.00	0.00	0.00	3,444.79	639,117.53	0.00	0.00	57.98	3,502.77
PORT LOUISA (11)*	0.00	0.00	0.00	0.00	47.50	16,000.00	0.00	0.00	22,575.88	22,623.38
UNION SLOUGH	0.00	0.00	0.00	0.00	2,845.24	210,406.69	70.70	608.00	0.00	2,915.94
TOTAL 2	0.00	0.00	0.00	0.00	6,337.53	865,524.22	70.70	608.00	22,633.86	29,042.09

	FISCAL YEAR MBCF ACQUISITION				CUMULATIVE TOTALS AT END OF FISCAL YEAR					
					MBCF					
	Purchased		Easement or Lease		Purchased		Easement or Lease		All Other	Total
State and Unit	Acres	Cost	Acres	Cost	Acres	Cost	Acres	Cost	Acres	Acres
KANSAS										
FLINT HILLS	0.00	0.00	0.00	0.00	0.00	0.00	0.00	0.00	18,463.36	18,463.36
FSA INTEREST KS** *	0.00	0.00	0.00	0.00	0.00	0.00	0.00	0.00	116.50	116.50
KIRWIN	0.00	0.00	0.00	0.00	0.00	0.00	0.00	0.00	10,778.00	10,778.00
QUIVIRA	0.00	0.00	0.00	0.00	21,820.10	2,059,238.00	0.00	0.00	199.20	22,019.30
TOTAL 3	0.00	0.00	0.00	0.00	21,820.10	2,059,238.00	0.00	0.00	29,557.06	51,377.16
KENTUCKY										
REELFOOT (14)	0.00	0.00	0.00	0.00	2,039.64	418,450.15	0.00	0.00	0.00	2,039.64
TOTAL 1	0.00	0.00	0.00	0.00	2,039.64	418,450.15	0.00	0.00	0.00	2,039.64
LOUISIANA										
BAYOU COCODRIE	0.00	0.00	0.00	0.00	3,363.60	2,016,578.00	0.00	0.00	9,804.91	13,168.51
CAMERON PRAIRIE	0.00	0.00	0.00	0.00	9,621.30	5,090,650.00	0.00	0.00	8,832.91	9,464.91
CAT ISLAND	0.00	0.00	0.00	0.00	632.00	500,000.00	0.00	0.00	1,722.91	2,354.91
CATAHOULA	0.00	0.00	0.00	0.00	14,789.86	2,130,082.25	0.00	0.00	10,119.75	24,909.61
D'ARBONNE	0.00	0.00	0.00	0.00	0.00	0.00	0.00	0.00	17,419.63	17,419.63
DELTA	0.00	0.00	0.00	0.00	34,462.73	233,324.17	0.00	0.00	14,336.37	48,799.10
FSA INTEREST LA** *	0.00	0.00	0.00	0.00	0.00	0.00	0.00	0.00	14,025.95	14,025.95
GRAND COTE	0.00	0.00	0.00	0.00	0.00	479,173.00	0.00	0.00	6,077.00	6,077.00
LACASSINE	0.00	0.00	0.00	12,800.00	9,886.29	999,156.43	652.51	186,300.00	23,839.97	34,378.77
LAKE OPHELIA	6.30	22,000.00	0.00	0.00	3,064.90	1,451,930.00	0.00	0.00	14,496.56	17,561.46
MANDALAY	0.00	0.00	0.00	0.00	0.00	0.00	0.00	0.00	4,619.00	4,619.00
RED RIVER	320.29	240,000	0.00	0.00	1,697.43	1,240,000.00	0.00	0.00	3,937.72	5,635.15
SABINE	0.00	0.00	0.00	0.00	566.66	14,000.51	0.00	0.00	125,223.42	125,790.08
UPPER OUACHITA	229.60	535,966.00	0.00	128,670.00	42,183.58	21,132,902.00	3,216.74	847,435.00	641.00	46,041.32
TOTAL 13	556.19	797,966.00	0.00	141,470.00	120,268.35	35,287,796.36	3,869.25	1,033,735.00	268,300.92	392,438.52
MAINE										
AROOSTOOK	0.00	0.00	0.00	0.00	0.00	0.00	0.00	0.00	4,655.07	4,655.07
CROSS ISLAND	0.00	0.00	0.00	0.00	0.00	0.00	0.00	0.00	1,703.10	1,703.10
FRANKLIN ISLAND	0.00	0.00	0.00	0.00	0.00	0.00	0.00	0.00	11.94	11.94
FSA INTEREST ME ***	0.00	0.00	0.00	0.00	0.00	0.00	0.00	0.00	622.08	622.08
LAKE UMBAGOG (36)*	0.00	0.00	0.00	0.00	1,519.40	426,970.00	0.00	0.00	3,034.28	4,553.68
MOOSEHORN	19.12	55,000.00	0.00	0.00	19,9782.52	2,051,582.19	0.00	2.00	9,086.54	28,869.06
PETIT MANAN	0.00	0.00	0.00	0.00	1,472.30	350,000.00	0.00	0.00	4,264.10	5,736.40
POND ISLAND	0.00	0.00	0.00	0.00	0.00	0.00	0.00	0.00	10.00	10.00
RACHEL CARSON	0.00	0.00	0.00	0.00	2,849.79	1,513,346.75	2.97	3,100.00	2,404.78	5,256.54
SEAL ISLAND	0.00	0.00	0.00	0.00	0.00	0.00	0.00	0.00	65.00	65.00
TOTAL 8	19.12	55,000.00	0.00	0.00	25,623.01	4,341,898.94	2.97	3,100.00	25,856.89	51,482.87
MARYLAND										
BLACKWATER	0.00	0.00	0.00	0.00	19,455.98	10,300,840.86	0.00	0.00	6,060.53	25,516.51
CHINCOTEAGUE(16)*	0.00	0.00	0.00	0.00	417.81	13,780.42	0.00	0.00	0.00	417.81
EASTERN NECK	0.00	0.00	0.00	0.00	2,286.27	1,606,145.09	0.00	0.00	0.00	2,286.27
FSA INTEREST MD ***	0.00	0.00	0.00	0.00	0.00	0.00	0.00	0.00	67.94	67.94
MARTIN (16)	0.00	0.00	0.00	0.00	1,853.57	61,027.00	0.00	0.00	2,569.86	4,423.43
PATUXENT	0.00	0.00	0.00	0.00	431.93	7,667.57	0.00	0.00	12,409.27	12,841.20
SUSQUEHANNA	0.00	0.00	0.00	0.00	0.00	0.00	0.00	0.00	3.79	3.79
TOTAL 5	0.00	0.00	0.00	0.00	24,445.56	11,989,460.94	0.00	0.00	21,111.39	45,556.95
MASSACHUSETTS										
ASSABET RIVER	0.00	0.00	0.00	0.00	0.00	0.00	0.00	0.00	2,229.20	2,229.20
GREAT MEADOWS	0.00	0.00	0.00	0.00	2,751.07	1,854,918.90	0.00	0.00	953.03	3,704.10
MONOMOY	0.00	0.00	0.00	0.00	2,665.71	18,339.00	0.00	0.00	36.14	2,701.85
NANTUCKET	0.00	0.00	0.00	0.00	0.00	0.00	0.00	0.00	39.80	39.80
NOMANS LAND ISLAND	0.00	0.00	0.00	0.00	0.00	0.00	0.00	0.00	628.00	628.00
OXBOW	0.00	0.00	0.00	0.00	0.00	0.00	0.00	0.00	1,672.32	1,672.32
PARKER RIVER	0.00	0.00	0.00	0.00	4,638.29	107,740.84	0.00	0.00	14.22	4,652.51
SILVIO O. CONTE (42)*	0.00	0.00	0.00	0.00	0.00	0.00	0.00	0.00	44.87	44.87
THACHER ISLAND	0.00	0.00	0.00	0.00	0.00	0.00	0.00	0.00	22.00	22.00
TOTAL 8	0.00	0.00	0.00	0.00	10,055.07	1,980,998.74	0.00	0.00	5,639.58	15,694.65

TABLE 1 - NATIONAL MIGRATORY BIRDS AREAS IN THE CONTERMINOUS UNITED STATES (continued)

State and Unit	FISCAL YEAR MBCF ACQUISITION				CUMULATIVE TOTALS AT END OF FISCAL YEAR					
	Purchased		Easement or Lease		MBCF				All Other	Total
					Purchased		Easement or Lease			
	Acres	Cost	Acres	Cost	Acres	Cost	Acres	Cost	Acres	Acres
MICHIGAN										
DETROIT RIVER	99.50	1,000,000.00	0.00	0.00	252.03	1,600,000.00	0.00	0.00	1,471.43	1,723.46
FSA INTEREST MI ***	0.00	0.00	0.00	0.00	0.00	0.00	0.00	0.00	94.00	94.00
MICHIGAN ISLANDS	0.00	0.00	0.00	0.00	0.00	0.00	0.00	0.00	597.39	597.39
SENEY	0.00	0.00	0.00	0.00	44,201.80	127,726.66	0.00	0.00	51,043.01	95,244.81
SHIAWASSEE	0.00	0.00	0.00	0.00	8,376.46	1,401,015.67	0.00	0.00	986.29	9,362.75
TOTAL 4	99.50	1,000,000.00	0.00	0.00	52,830.29	3,128,742.33	0.00	0.00	54,192.12	107,022.41
MINNESOTA										
AGASSIZ	0.00	0.00	0.00	0.00	700.11	40,226.04	0.00	0.00	60,800.82	61,500.93
BIG STONE	0.00	0.00	0.00	0.00	0.00	0.00	0.00	0.00	11,520.13	11,520.13
FSA INTEREST MN ***	0.00	0.00	0.00	0.00	0.00	0.00	0.00	0.00	2,561.80	2,561.80
HAMDEN SLOUGH	0.00	0.00	0.00	0.00	3,073.10	1,832,872.00	0.00	0.00	136.75	3,209.85
RICE LAKE	0.00	0.00	0.00	0.00	6,435.60	197,329.77	0.00	0.00	10,036.68	16,472.28
RYDELL	0.00	0.00	0.00	0.00	0.00	0.00	0.00	0.00	2,070.00	2,070.00
SHERBURNE	0.00	0.00	0.00	0.00	29,556.90	3,273,341.05	0.00	0.00	120.94	29,677.84
TAMARAC	0.00	0.00	0.00	0.00	35,151.38	612,159.93	0.00	0.00	40.00	35,191.38
TOTAL 7	0.00	0.00	0.00	0.00	74,917.09	5,955,928.79	0.00	0.00	87,287.12	162,204.21
MISSISSIPPI										
COLDWATER RIVER	0.00	0.00	0.00	0.00	2,374.10	1,430,450.00	0.00	0.00	94.26	2,468.36
DAHOMEY	0.00	0.00	0.00	2,600.00	0.00	0.00	260.00	2,600.00	8,906.80	9,166.80
FSA INTEREST MS ***	0.00	0.00	0.00	0.00	0.00	0.00	0.00	0.00	20,715.69	20,715.69
HILLSIDE	0.00	0.00	0.00	0.00	3,644.02	2,877,600.00	0.00	0.00	15,407.37	19,051.39
MATHEWS BRAKE	0.00	0.00	0.00	0.00	2,418.74	1,691,446.00	0.00	0.00	0.00	2,418.74
MORGAN BRAKE	0.00	0.00	0.00	0.00	7,241.28	4,517,482.20	0.00	0.00	131.83	7,373.11
NOXUBEE	0.00	0.00	0.00	0.00	1,412.34	145,413.05	0.00	0.00	45,636.85	47,049.19
PANTHER SWAMP	0.00	0.00	0.00	16,032.00	27,556.19	14,990,723.00	640.00	108,678.00	7,075.66	35,271.85
ST. CATHERINE CREEK	0.00	0.00	0.00	5,523.10	24,429.29	12,925,167.00	502.10	39,686.02	0.00	24,931.39
TALLAHATCHIE	0.00	0.00	0.00	0.00	2,324.14	1,361,000.00	0.00	0.00	470.00	2,794.14
YAZOO	0.00	0.00	0.00	0.00	12,940.43	2,692,503.78	0.00	0.00	2.21	12,942.64
TOTAL 10	0.00	0.00	0.00	24,155.10	84,340.53	42,631,785.03	1,402.10	150,964.02	98,440.67	184,18.30
MISSOURI										
CLARENCE CANNON	0.00	0.00	0.00	0.00	3,736.04	1,163,649.25	0.00	0.00	13.94	3,749.98
FSA INTEREST MO ***	0.00	0.00	0.00	0.00	0.00	0.00	0.00	0.00	1,784.68	1,784.68
GREAT RIVER (11)*	0.00	0.00	0.00	0.00	1,119.78	460,000.00	0.00	0.00	988.15	2,107.93
MIDDLE MISSISSIPPI										
RIVER (11)*	0.00	0.00	0.00	0.00	0.00	0.00	0.00	0.00	1,704.17	1,704.17
MINGO	0.00	0.00	0.00	0.00	21,620.76	298,615.82	11.86	27.00	113.24	21,745.86
SQUAW CREEK	0.00	0.00	0.00	0.00	801.32	38,275.46	1.00	0.00	6,612.57	7,414.89
SWAN LAKE	0.00	0.00	0.00	0.00	5,379.32	355,194.19	0.00	0.00	6,11.3.65	11,492.97
TWO RIVERS (11)*	0.00	0.00	0.00	0.00	0.00	0.00	0.00	0.00	232.00	232.00
TOTAL 4	0.00	0.00	0.00	0.00	32,657.22	2,315,733.72	12.86	27.00	17,562.40	50,232.48
MONTANA										
BENTON LAKE	0.00	0.00	0.00	0.00	147.64	5,315.00	68.69	8,763.00	12,243.11	12,459.44
BLACK COULEE	0.00	0.00	0.00	0.00	0.00	0.00	0.00	0.00	1,308.88	1,308.88
BOWDOIN	0.00	0.00	0.00	0.00	0.00	0.00	0.00	0.00	15,551.97	15,551.97
CHARLES M. RUSSELL	0.00	0.00	0.00	0.00	0.00	0.00	0.00	0.00	913,214.22	913,214.22
CREEDMAN COULEE	0.00	0.00	0.00	0.00	0.00	0.00	0.00	0.00	2,728.00	2,728.00
FSA INTEREST MT ***	0.00	0.00	0.00	0.00	0.00	0.00	0.00	0.00	510.62	510.62
HAILSTONE	0.00	0.00	0.00	0.00	0.00	0.00	0.00	0.00	920.00	920.00
HALFBREED LAKE	0.00	0.00	0.00	1,512.00	3,279.02	291,000.00	1,039.22	25,890.20	0.00	4,318.24
HEWITT LAKE	0.00	0.00	0.00	0.00	0.00	0.00	0.00	0.00	1,360.92	1,360.92
LAKE MASON	0.00	0.00	0.00	0.00	4,100.45	0.00	0.00	0.00	12,714.07	16,814.52
LAKE THIBADEAU	0.00	0.00	0.00	0.00	0.00	0.00	0.00	0.00	3,868.48	3,868.48
LAMESTEER	0.00	0.00	0.00	0.00	0.00	0.00	0.00	0.00	800.00	800.00
LEE METCALF	0.00	0.00	0.00	0.00	2,696.29	799,680.00	0.00	0.00	96.23	2,792.52
LOST TRAIL	0.00	0.00	0.00	1,184.56	4,693.20	1,728,205.00	1,029.04	4,849.78	3,112.00	8,834.24
MEDICINE LAKE	0.00	0.00	0.00	0.00	2,513.26	25,460.00	0.00	0.00	29,020.45	31,533.71
RED ROCK LAKES	0.00	0.00	0.00	0.00	1,024.75	70,109.00	0.00	0.00	57,301.69	58,326.44
SWAN RIVER	0.00	0.00	0.00	0.00	1,568.81	901,645.00	0.00	0.00	0.00	1,568.81
UL BEND	0.00	0.00	0.00	0.00	9,688.19	577,280.00	0.00	0.00	46,361.37	56,049.56
WAR HORSE	0.00	0.00	0.00	0.00	0.00	0.00	0.00	0.00	3,392.87	3,392.87
TOTAL 18	0.00	0.00	0.00	2,96.56	29,711.61	4,398,694.00	2,136.95	39,502.98	1,104,504.88	1,136,353.44

	FISCAL YEAR MBCF ACQUISITION				CUMULATIVE TOTALS AT END OF FISCAL YEAR					
	Purchased		Easement or Lease		MBCF					
					Purchased		Easement or Lease		All Other	Total
State and Unit	Acres	Cost	Acres	Cost	Acres	Cost	Acres	Cost	Acres	Acres
NEBRASKA										
CRESCENT LAKE	0.00	0.00	0.00	0.00	5,184.55	31,048.00	31.49	3,189.00	39,389.31	45,995.35
DeSOTO (19)*	0.00	0.00	0.00	0.00	3,660.32	591,507.20	0.00	0.00	663.88	4,324.20
FSA INTEREST NE ***	0.00	0.00	0.00	0.00	0.00	0.00	0.00	0.00	2,092.72	2,092.72
VALENTINE	0.00	0.00	0.00	0.00	5,078.34	62,747.00	0.00	0.00	68,019.75	73,098.09
TOTAL 2	0.00	0.00	0.00	0.00	13,923.21	685,302.20	31.49	3,189.00	111,555.66	125,510.36
NEVADA										
ANAHO ISLAND	0.00	0.00	0.00	0.00	0.00	0.00	0.00	0.00	247.73	247.73
DESERT	0.00	0.00	0.00	0.00	320.00	5,600.00	0.00	250.00	1,615,001.39	1,615,321.39
FALLON	0.00	0.00	0.00	0.00	0.00	0.00	0.00	0.00	17,901.94	17,901.94
PAHRANAGAT	0.00	0.00	0.00	0.00	3,915.60	500,000.00	0.75	0.00	1,466.39	5,382.74
RUBY LAKE	0.00	0.00	0.00	0.00	29,945.73	208,437.25	0.00	0.00	9,340.37	39,286.10
SHELDON (4)	0.00	0.00	0.00	0.00	23,143.67	2,002.00	0.00	0.00	549,732.48	572,876.15
STILLWATER	0.00	0.00	0.00	0.00	0.00	0.00	0.00	0.00	87,564.52	87,564.52
TOTAL 7	0.00	0.00	0.00	0.00	57,325.00	716,039.25	0.75	250.00	2,281,254.82	2,338,580.57
NEW HAMPSHIRE										
LAKE UMBAGOG (37)	0.00	0.00	0.00	0.00	5,357.59	2,128,275.00	0.00	0.00	7,789.33	13,146.92
SILVIO O. CONTE (43)*	0.00	0.00	0.00	0.00	0.00	0.00	0.00	0.00	3,680.82	3,680.82
TOTAL 1	0.00	0.00	0.00	0.00	5,357.59	2,128,275.00	0.00	0.00	11,470.15	16,827.74
NEW JERSEY										
CAPE MAY NWR	72.11	40,677.00	0.00	0.00	4,488.33	4,969,520.00	0.00	0.00	6,648.94	11,137.27
EDWIN B. FORSYTHE	220.76	211,340.00	0.00	0.00	39,398.49	16,451,290.97	0.00	1,300.00	6,920.78	46,319.27
GREAT SWAMP	0.00	0.00	0.00	0.00	2,808.67	3,577,691.05	0.00	1.00	4,789.69	7,598.36
SUPAWNA MEADOWS	0.00	0.00	0.00	0.00	2,526.83	968,744.00	0.00	0.00	367.92	2,894.75
WALLKILL RIVER (39)	0.00	0.00	0.00	0.00	1,214.21	2,535,665.00	0.00	0.00	3,530.72	4,744.93
TOTAL 5	292.87	252,017.00	0.00	0.00	50,436.53	28,502,911.02	0.00	1,300.00	22,258.05	72,694.58
NEW MEXICO										
BITTER LAKE	0.00	0.00	0.00	0.00	10,753.66	52,304.00	0.00	0.00	13,854.98	24,608.64
BOSQUE DEL APACHE	0.00	0.00	0.00	0.00	56,850.31	125,311.00	0.00	0.00	340.79	57,191.10
LAS VEGAS	0.00	0.00	0.00	0.00	8,672.08	2,121,150.00	0.00	0.00	0.00	8,672.08
MAXWELL	0.00	0.00	0.00	0.00	2,791.69	423,370.79	0.00	0.00	906.90	3,698.59
TOTAL 4	0.00	0.00	0.00	0.00	79,067.74	2,722,135.79	0.00	0.00	15,102.67	94,170.41
NEW YORK										
AMAGANSETT	0.00	0.00	0.00	0.00	0.00	0.00	0.00	0.00	35.84	35.84
CONSCIENCE POINT	0.00	0.00	0.00	0.00	0.00	0.00	0.00	0.00	60.40	60.40
ELIZABETH A. MORTON	0.00	0.00	0.00	0.00	0.00	0.00	0.00	0.00	187.19	187.19
FSA INTEREST NY ** *	0.00	0.00	0.00	0.00	0.00	0.00	0.00	0.00	2,714.10	2,714.10
IROQUOIS	0.00	0.00	0.00	0.00	10,757.81	1,279,615.46	0.00	0.00	70.25	10,828.06
MONTEZUMA	0.00	0.00	0.00	0.00	7,510.72	2,014,906.56	0.00	0.00	946.32	8,457.04
OYSTER BAY	0.00	0.00	0.00	0.00	0.00	0.00	0.00	0.00	3,204.08	3,204.08
SEATUCK	0.00	0.00	0.00	0.00	0.00	0.00	0.00	0.00	209.23	209.23
SHAWANGUNK GRASSLANDS	0.00	0.00	0.00	0.00	0.00	0.00	0.00	0.00	566.53	566.53
TARGET ROCK	0.00	0.00	0.00	0.00	0.00	0.00	0.00	0.00	80.09	80.09
WALLKILL RIVER (40)	0.00	0.00	0.00	0.00	0.00	0.00	0.00	0.00	147.09	147.09
WERTHEIM	0.00	0.00	0.00	0.00	188.70	193,217.80	0.00	0.00	2,380.66	2,569.36
TOTAL 11	0.00	0.00	0.00	0.00	18,457.23	3,487,739.82	0.00	0.00	10,601.78	29,059.01
NORTH CAROLINA										
CEDAR ISLAND	0.00	0.00	0.00	0.00	12,484.77	347,171.21	0.00	0.00	1,997.55	14,482.32
CURRITUCK	0.00	0.00	0.00	0.00	3,763.79	8,689,434.00	225.76	120,000.00	4,324.09	8,313.64
FSA INTEREST NC ***	0.00	0.00	0.00	0.00	0.00	0.00	0.00	0.00	6,434.04	6,434.04
GREAT DISMAL SWAMP (16)	0.00	0.00	0.00	0.00	0.00	0.00	0.00	0.00	24,811.80	26,109.70
MACKAY ISLAND (16)	0.00	0.00	0.00	0.00	6,348.15	953,306.95	0.00	0.00	996.61	7,344.76
MATTAMUSKEET	0.00	0.00	0.00	0.00	252.04	1,285.35	0.00	0.00	49,928.14	50,180.18
PEA ISLAND	0.00	0.00	0.00	0.00	5,787.97	40,401.86	0.00	0.00	46.23	5,834.20
PEE DEE	0.00	0.00	0.00	0.00	8,438.94	2,561,851.76	0.00	0.00	0.00	8,438.94
POCOSIN LAKES	0.00	0.00	0.00	0.00	12,350.35	1,682,157.99	0.00	0.00	97,756.29	110,106.64
ROANOKE RIVER	1,584.63	0.00	0.00	0.00	13,106.63	6,345,258.00	0.00	0.00	4,870.00	17,976.63
SWANQUARTER	0.00	0.00	0.00	0.00	15,492.76	60,920.93	0.00	0.00	918.33	16,411.09
TOTAL 10	1,584.63	993,000.00	0.00	0.00	82,409.10	23,786,968.05	225.76	120,000.00	192,354.82	274,717.94

TABLE 1 - NATIONAL MIGRATORY BIRDS AREAS IN THE CONTERMINOUS UNITED STATES (continued)

	FISCAL YEAR MBCF ACQUISITION				CUMULATIVE TOTALS AT END OF FISCAL YEAR					
					MBCF					
	Purchased		Easement or Lease		Purchased		Easement or Lease		All Other	Total
State and Unit	Acres	Cost	Acres	Cost	Acres	Cost	Acres	Cost	Acres	Acres
NORTH DAKOTA										
APPERT LAKE	0.00	0.00	0.00	0.00	0.00	0.00	0.00	0.00	907.75	907.75
ARDOCH	0.00	0.00	0.00	0.00	288.13	2,739.00	0.00	0.00	2,408.00	2,696.13
ARROWWOOD	0.00	0.00	0.00	0.00	2,097.51	46,906.58	0.00	0.00	13,845.35	15,942.86
AUDUBON	0.00	0.00	0.00	0.00	0.00	0.00	0.00	0.00	14,739.19	14,739.19
BONE HILL	0.00	0.00	0.00	0.00	0.00	0.00	0.00	0.00	640.00	640.00
BRUMBA	0.00	0.00	0.00	0.00	0.00	0.00	0.00	0.00	1,977.48	1,977.48
BUFFALO LAKE	0.00	0.00	0.00	0.00	0.00	0.00	0.00	0.00	1,563.72	1,563.72
CAMP LAKE	0.00	0.00	0.00	0.00	0.00	0.00	0.00	0.00	584.70	584.70
CANFIELD LAKE	0.00	0.00	0.00	0.00	3.10	100.00	0.00	0.00	310.13	313.23
CHASE LAKE	0.00	0.00	0.00	0.00	4,449.47	25,611.00	0.00	0.00	0.00	4,449.47
COTTONWOOD LAKE	0.00	0.00	0.00	0.00	0.00	0.00	0.00	0.00	1,013.47	1,013.47
DAKOTA LAKE	0.00	0.00	0.00	0.00	0.00	0.00	0.00	0.00	2,799.78	2,799.78
DES LACS	0.00	0.00	0.00	0.00	701.82	6,893.60	2.70	0.00	18,842.62	19,547.14
FLORENCE LAKE	0.00	0.00	0.00	0.00	1,468.40	31,485.00	0.00	0.00	419.80	1,888.20
FSA INTEREST ND ***	0.00	0.00	0.00	0.00	0.00	0.00	0.00	0.00	6,591.40	6,591.40
HALF-WAY LAKE	0.00	0.00	0.00	0.00	0.00	0.00	160.00	0.00	0.00	160.00
HIDDENWOOD	0.00	0.00	0.00	0.00	0.00	0.00	568.35	0.00	0.00	568.35
HOBART LAKE	0.00	0.00	0.00	0.00	236.49	5,165.00	0.00	0.00	1,840.61	2,077.10
HUTCHINSON LAKE	0.00	0.00	0.00	0.00	0.00	0.00	0.00	0.00	478.90	478.90
J. CLARK SALYER	0.00	0.00	0.00	0.00	21,648.66	306,352.60	50.52	0.00	37,675.93	59,375.11
JOHNSON LAKE	0.00	0.00	0.00	0.00	0.00	0.00	0.00	0.00	2,007.91	2,007.91
KELLYS SLOUGH	0.00	0.00	0.00	0.00	0.00	0.00	0.00	0.00	1,269.50	1,269.50
LAKE ALICE	0.00	0.00	0.00	0.00	8,027.86	2,067,184.00	8.00	0.00	4,059.68	12,095.54
LAKE GEORGE	0.00	0.00	0.00	0.00	0.00	0.00	0.00	0.00	3,118.81	3,118.81
LAKE ILO	0.00	0.00	0.00	0.00	3,178.30	78,582.98	0.00	0.00	854.82	4,033.12
LAKE NETTIE	0.00	0.00	0.00	0.00	2,420.60	148,245.00	0.00	0.00	634.30	3,054.90
LAKE OTIS	0.00	0.00	0.00	0.00	0.00	0.00	0.00	0.00	320.00	320.00
LAKE PATRICIA	0.00	0.00	0.00	0.00	0.00	0.00	0.00	0.00	800.23	800.23
LAKE ZAHL	0.00	0.00	0.00	0.00	3,178.98	53,275.00	0.00	0.00	644.21	3,823.19
LAMBS LAKE	0.00	0.00	0.00	0.00	0.00	0.00	0.00	0.00	1,206.67	1,206.67
LITTLE GOOSE	0.00	0.00	0.00	0.00	0.00	0.00	0.00	0.00	288.41	288.41
LONG LAKE	0.00	0.00	0.00	0.00	12,578.82	77,180.00	217.35	10.00	9,702.33	22,498.50
LORDS LAKE	0.00	0.00	0.00	0.00	0.00	0.00	0.00	0.00	1,915.29	1,915.29
LOST LAKE	0.00	0.00	0.00	0.00	0.00	0.00	0.00	0.00	960.21	960.21
LOSTWOOD	0.00	0.00	0.00	0.00	3,148.01	24,553.00	0.00	0.00	23,755.98	26,903.99
MAPLE RIVER	0.00	0.00	0.00	0.00	0.00	0.00	0.00	0.00	712.00	712.00
MCLEAN	0.00	0.00	0.00	0.00	344.00	12,516.00	0.00	0.00	416.00	760.00
PLEASANT LAKE	0.00	0.00	0.00	0.00	0.00	0.00	0.00	0.00	897.80	897.80
PRETTY ROCK	0.00	0.00	0.00	0.00	0.00	0.00	0.00	0.00	800.00	800.00
RABB LAKE	0.00	0.00	0.00	0.00	0.00	0.00	0.00	0.00	260.80	260.80
ROCK LAKE	0.00	0.00	0.00	0.00	0.00	0.00	0.00	0.00	5,505.96	5,505.96
ROSE LAKE	0.00	0.00	0.00	0.00	0.00	0.00	0.00	0.00	836.30	836.30
SCHOOL SECTION LAKE	0.00	0.00	0.00	0.00	0.00	0.00	0.00	0.00	297.30	297.30
SHELL LAKE	0.00	0.00	0.00	0.00	710.20	17,902.00	0.00	0.00	1,124.90	1,835.10
SHEYENNE LAKE	0.00	0.00	0.00	0.00	0.00	0.00	0.00	0.00	797.30	797.30
SIBLEY LAKE	0.00	0.00	0.00	0.00	0.00	0.00	0.00	0.00	1,077.40	1,077.40
SILVER LAKE	0.00	0.00	0.00	0.00	0.00	0.00	0.00	0.00	3,347.64	3,347.64
SLADE	0.00	0.00	0.00	0.00	0.00	0.00	0.00	0.00	3,000.20	3,000.20
SNYDER LAKE	0.00	0.00	0.00	0.00	0.00	0.00	0.00	0.00	1,550.18	1,550.18
SPRINGWATER	0.00	0.00	0.00	0.00	0.00	0.00	0.00	0.00	640.00	640.00
STEWART LAKE	0.00	0.00	0.00	0.00	0.00	0.00	0.00	0.00	2,230.40	2,230.40
STONEY SLOUGH	0.00	0.00	0.00	0.00	0.00	0.00	0.00	0.00	880.00	880.00
STORM LAKE	0.00	0.00	0.00	0.00	0.00	0.00	0.00	0.00	685.90	685.90
STUMP LAKE	0.00	0.00	0.00	0.00	0.00	0.00	0.00	0.00	27.39	27.39
SUNBURST LAKE	0.00	0.00	0.00	0.00	0.00	0.00	0.00	0.00	327.51	327.51
TEWAUKON	0.00	0.00	0.00	0.00	6,856.65	460,124.00	0.00	0.00	1,807.32	8,363.62
TOMAHAWK	0.00	0.00	0.00	0.00	0.00	0.00	0.00	0.00	440.00	440.00
UPPER SOURIS	0.00	0.00	0.00	0.00	2,900.81	41,220.00	0.00	0.00	29,401.44	32,302.25
WHITE LAKE	0.00	0.00	0.00	0.00	1,040.00	28,800.00	0.00	0.00	0.00	1,040.00
WILD RICE LAKE	0.00	0.00	0.00	0.00	0.00	0.00	0.00	0.00	778.80	778.80
WILLOW LAKE	0.00	0.00	0.00	0.00	0.00	0.00	0.00	0.00	2,620.38	2,620.38
WINTERING RIVER	0.00	0.00	0.00	0.00	0.00	0.00	0.00	0.00	239.26	239.26
WOOD LAKE	0.00	0.00	0.00	0.00	0.00	0.00	0.00	0.00	280.00	280.00
TOTAL 62	0.00	0.00	0.00	0.00	74,907.27	3,434,832.76	1,006.92	10.00	219,229.55	295,143.74

TABLE 1 - NATIONAL MIGRATORY BIRDS AREAS IN THE CONTERMINOUS UNITED STATES (continued)

State and Unit	FISCAL YEAR MBCF ACQUISITION				CUMULATIVE TOTALS AT END OF FISCAL YEAR					
	Purchased		Easement or Lease		MBCF				All Other	Total
					Purchased		Easement or Lease			
	Acres	Cost	Acres	Cost	Acres	Cost	Acres	Cost	Acres	Acres
OHIO										
CEDAR POINT	0.00	0.00	0.00	0.00	0.00	0.00	0.00	0.00	2,449.77	2,449.77
OTTAWA	72.56	160,800.00	0.00	0.00	5,244.67	2,733,693.55	590.80	2.00	595.58	6,431.05
WEST SISTER ISLAND	0.00	0.00	0.00	0.00	0.00	0.00	0.00	0.00	80.13	80.13
TOTAL 3	72.56	160,800.00	0.00	0.00	5,244.67	2,733,693.55	590.80	2.00	3,125.48	8,960.95
OKLAHOMA										
DEEP FORK	0.00	0.00	0.00	0.00	1,571.50	421,000.00	0.00	0.00	7,207.84	8,779.34
LITTLE RIVER	0.00	0.00	0.00	0.00	12,262.16	9,881,540.94	0.00	0.00	1,337.88	13,600.04
OPTIMA	0.00	0.00	0.00	0.00	0.00	0.00	0.00	0.00	4,332.81	4,332.81
SALT PLAINS	0.00	0.00	0.00	0.00	1,117.39	50,837.00	0.00	0.00	30,939.73	32,057.12
SEQUOYAH	0.00	0.00	0.00	0.00	0.00	0.00	0.00	0.00	20,800.00	20,800.00
TISHOMINGO	0.00	0.00	0.00	0.00	0.00	0.00	0.00	0.00	16,464.18	16,464.18
WASHITA	0.00	0.00	0.00	0.00	0.00	0.00	0.00	1.00	8,075.37	8,075.37
TOTAL 7	0.00	0.00	0.00	0.00	14,951.05	10,353,377.94	0.00	1.00	89,157.81	104,108.86
OREGON										
ANKENY	0.00	0.00	0.00	0.00	2,796.33	893,600.00	0.00	0.00	0.00	2,796.33
BASKETT SLOUGH	0.00	0.00	0.00	0.00	2,492.33	941,985.00	0.00	0.00	0.00	2,492.33
CAPE MEARES	0.00	0.00	0.00	0.00	0.00	0.00	0.00	0.00	138.51	138.51
COLD SPRINGS	0.00	0.00	0.00	0.00	386.88	2,760.00	0.00	0.00	2,729.95	3,116.83
DEER FLAT (21)*	0.00	0.00	0.00	0.00	0.00	0.00	0.00	0.00	187.94	187.94
HART MOUNTAIN	0.00	0.00	0.00	0.00	54,837.26	216,114.58	0.00	0.00	215,086.32	269,923.58
KLAMATH MARSH	0.00	0.00	0.00	0.00	18,288.86	2,070,694.00	0.00	0.00	22,596.12	40,884.98
LEWIS AND CLARK	0.00	0.00	0.00	0.00	2,850.63	469,250.00	0.00	0.00	9,316.22	12,166.85
LOWER KLAMATH (2) *	0.00	0.00	0.00	0.00	0.00	0.00	0.00	0.00	6,618.13	6,618.13
MALHEUR	0.00	0.00	0.00	0.00	47,953.58	2,461,939.35	0.00	0.00	139,173.36	187,126.94
OREGON ISLANDS	0.00	0.00	0.00	0.00	0.00	0.00	0.00	0.00	1,079.61	1,079.61
SHELDON (15)*	0.00	0.00	0.00	0.00	627.48	4,079.00	0.00	0.00	0.00	627.48
UMATILLA (26)	0.00	0.00	0.00	0.00	0.00	0.00	0.00	0.00	8,907.37	8,907.37
UPPER KLAMATH	0.00	0.00	0.00	0.00	4,146.10	123,476.00	0.00	0.00	10,820.06	14,966.16
WILLIAM L. FINLEY	0.00	0.00	0.00	0.00	5,665.96	2,480,800.00	7.15	0.00	0.00	5,673.11
TOTAL 12	0.00	0.00	0.00	0.00	140,045.41	9,664,697.93	7.15	0.00	417,260.64	557,313.20
PENNSYLVANIA										
ERIE	0.00	0.00	0.00	0.00	7,962.81	911,480.12	0.00	0.00	837.42	8,800.23
JOHN HEINZ	0.00	0.00	0.00	0.00	80.33	20,966.00	0.00	0.00	912.84	993.17
TOTAL 2	0.00	0.00	0.00	0.00	8,043.14	932,446.12	0.00	0.00	1,750.26	9,793.40
RHODE ISLAND										
BLOCK ISLAND	0.00	0.00	0.00	0.00	0.00	0.00	0.00	0.00	128.92	128.92
JOHN H. CHAFEE	0.00	0.00	0.00	0.00	0.00	0.00	0.00	0.00	427.90	427.90
NINIGRET	0.00	0.00	0.00	0.00	0.00	0.00	0.00	0.00	866.94	866.94
SACHUEST POINT	0.00	0.00	0.00	0.00	0.00	0.00	0.00	0.00	241.90	241.90
TRUSTOM POND	0.00	0.00	0.00	0.00	0.00	0.00	0.00	0.00	777.30	777.30
TOTAL 5	0.00	0.00	0.00	0.00	0.00	0.00	0.00	0.00	2,442.96	2,442.96
SOUTH CAROLINA										
CAPE ROMAIN	0.00	0.00	0.00	0.00	22,237.29	17,218.18	0.00	0.00	43,031.37	65,268.66
CAROLINA SANDHILLS	0.00	0.00	0.00	0.00	580.20	38,352.75	0.00	0.00	44,856.23	45,436.43
FSA INTEREST SC ***	0.00	0.00	0.00	0.00	0.00	0.00	0.00	0.00	1,430.04	1,430.04
PINCKNEY ISLAND	0.00	0.00	0.00	0.00	0.00	0.00	0.00	0.00	4,052.70	4,052.70
SANTEE	0.00	0.00	0.00	0.00	4,322.43	549,953.57	0.00	0.00	8,160.85	12,483.28
SAVANNAH (1) *	0.00	0.00	0.00	0.00	7,540.29	1,462,058.30	0.00	0.00	7,471.08	15,011.37
TYBEE	0.00	0.00	0.00	0.00	0.00	0.00	0.00	0.00	100.00	100.00
TOTAL 5	0.00	0.00	0.00	0.00	34,680.21	2,067,582.80	0.00	0.00	109,102.27	143,782.48
SOUTH DAKOTA										
BEAR BUTTE	0.00	0.00	0.00	0.00	0.00	0.00	0.00	0.00	374.20	374.20
FSA INTEREST SD ***	0.00	0.00	0.00	0.00	0.00	0.00	0.00	0.00	151.20	151.20
LACREEK	0.00	0.00	0.00	0.00	9,379.75	788,491.00	80.00	15,933.00	7,395.58	16,855.33
LAKE ANDES	0.00	0.00	0.00	0.00	617.64	92,322.00	0.00	0.00	5,021.79	5,639.43
SAND LAKE	0.00	0.00	0.00	0.00	3,917.39	90,622.00	0.00	0.00	17,902.80	21,820.19
WAUBAY	0.00	0.00	0.00	0.00	683.77	23,838.00	90.53	0.00	3,965.92	4,740.22
TOTAL 5	0.00	0.00	0.00	0.00	14,598.55	995,273.00	170.53	15,933.00	34,811.49	49,580.57

TABLE 1 - NATIONAL MIGRATORY BIRDS AREAS IN THE CONTERMINOUS UNITED STATES (continued)

State and Unit	FISCAL YEAR MBCF ACQUISITION				CUMULATIVE TOTALS AT END OF FISCAL YEAR					
	Purchased		Easement or Lease		MBCF				All Other	Total
					Purchased		Easement or Lease			
	Acres	Cost	Acres	Cost	Acres	Cost	Acres	Cost	Acres	Acres
TENNESSEE										
CHICKASAW	254.43	625,773.00	0.00	0.00	15,299.59	17,686,888.72	0.00	0.00	9,589.45	24,889.04
CROSS CREEKS	0.00	0.00	0.00	0.00	87.64	26,200.00	0.00	0.00	8,773.85	8,861.49
FSA INTEREST TN ***	0.00	0.00	0.00	0.00	0.00	0.00	0.00	0.00	685.39	685.39
HATCHIE	0.00	0.00	0.00	0.00	11,220.73	1,862,329.25	0.00	0.00	335.37	11,556.10
LAKE ISOM	0.00	0.00	0.00	0.00	344.65	27,290.72	0.00	0.00	1,501.31	1,845.96
LOWER HATCHIE	0.00	0.00	0.00	0.00	8,492.48	11,163,126.00	0.00	0.00	2,701.52	11,194.00
REELFOOT (22)*	0.00	0.00	0.00	0.00	496.53	109,531.78	0.00	0.00	7,914.21	8,410.74
TENNESSEE	0.00	0.00	0.00	0.00	430.45	72,151.10	0.00	0.00	50,929.01	51,359.46
TOTAL 6	254.43	625,773.00	0.00	0.00	36,372.07	30,947,517.57	0.00	0.00	82,430.11	118,802.18
TEXAS										
ANAHUAC	0.00	0.00	0.00	0.00	29,924.39	12,440,153.40	63.09	0.00	4,308.75	34,296.23
ARANSAS	0.00	0.00	0.00	0.00	49,235.68	1,833,531.80	0.00	0.00	65,176.40	114,412.08
BIG BOGGY	0.00	0.00	0.00	0.00	4,113.41	2,374,594.19	258.23	58,112.00	154.53	4,526.17
BRAZORIA	0.00	0.00	0.00	0.00	42,641.23	13,822,482.26	0.00	0.00	1,772.65	44,413.88
BUFFALO LAKE	0.00	0.00	0.00	0.00	0.00	0.00	0.00	0.00	7,664.16	7,664.16
FSA INTEREST TX ***	0.00	0.00	0.00	0.00	0.00	0.00	0.00	0.00	1,878.13	1,878.13
HAGERMAN	0.00	0.00	0.00	0.00	0.00	0.00	0.00	0.00	11,319.84	11,319.84
LAGUNA ATASCOSA	0.00	0.00	0.00	0.00	77,311.68	12,475,079.19	0.00	0.00	9,506.24	86,817.92
LITTLE SANDY	0.00	0.00	0.00	0.00	0.00	0.00	3,802.00	0.00	0.00	3,802.00
MCFADDIN	0.00	0.00	0.00	0.00	48,431.82	10,219,300.00	7,748.88	1,394,170.00	0.00	56,180.70
MOODY	0.00	0.00	0.00	0.00	0.00	0.00	3,516.87	0.00	0.00	3,516.87
MULESHOE	0.00	0.00	0.00	0.00	2,154.80	25,740.00	0.00	0.00	3,654.30	5,809.10
SAN BERNARD	203.26	914,670.00	0.00	0.00	29,076.07	9,550,967.32	0.00	0.00	7,758.94	36,835.01
SANTA ANA	0.00	0.00	0.00	0.00	1,980.50	23,766.00	0.00	0.00	107.00	2,087.50
TEXAS POINT	0.00	0.00	0.00	0.00	8,952.02	1,719,000.00	0.00	0.00	0.00	8,952.02
TRINITY RIVER	453.81	213,296.81	0.00	0.00	9,617.82	5,974,172.81	0.00	0.00	8,615.73	18,233.55
TOTAL 15	657.07	1,127,966.81	0.00	0.00	303,439.42	70,458,786.42	15,389.07	1,452,282.00	121,916.67	440,745.16
UTAH										
BEAR RIVER	0.00	0.00	0.00	0.00	25,829.01	3,579,119.47	46.64	740.00.00	47,889.74	73,765.39
FISH SPRINGS	0.00	0.00	0.00	0.00	3,774.82	93,325.00	0.00	73.00	14,217.42	17,992.24
FSA INTEREST UT ***	0.00	0.00	0.00	0.00	0.00	0.00	0.00	0.00	280.84	280.84
OURAY	0.00	0.00	0.00	18,750.00	5,014.98	487,084.25	3,844.68	331,727.92	3,278.58	12,138.24
TOTAL 3	0.00	0.00	0.00	18,750.00	34,618.81	4,159,528.72	3,891.32	332,540.92	65,666.58	104,176.71
VERMONT										
FSA INTEREST VT ***	0.00	0.00	0.00	0.00	0.00	0.00	0.00	0.00	71.00	71.00
MISSISQUOI	0.00	0.00	0.00	0.00	6,155.14	291,134.27	0.00	0.00	405.34	6,560.48
SILVIO O. CONTE (41)	0.00	0.00	0.00	0.00	17,112.31	4,278,574.00	0.00	0.00	9,421.80	26,534.11
TOTAL 2	0.00	0.00	0.00	0.00	23,267.45	4,569,708.27	0.00	0.00	9,898.14	33,165.59
VIRGINIA										
BACK BAY	0.00	0.00	0.00	0.00	7,389.42	5,160,662.00	0.00	0.00	1,498.22	8,980.64
CHINCOTEAGUE (23)	0.00	0.00	0.00	0.00	9,513.02	635,403.91	0.00	0.00	4,101.66	13,614.68
EASTERN SHORE OF VIRGINIA	0.00	0.00	0.00	0.00	375.80	1,058,000.00	0.00	0.00	747.47	1,123.27
FISHERMAN ISLAND	0.00	0.00	0.00	0.00	825.00	1,600,000.00	0.00	0.00	1,071.30	1,896.30
FSA INTEREST VA ***	0.00	0.00	0.00	0.00	0.00	0.00	0.00	0.00	133.70	133.70
GREAT DISMAL SWAMP (24)*	0.00	0.00	0.00	0.00	2,896.42	2,824,762.98	0.00	0.00	82,196.69	85,093.11
MACKAY ISLAND (24)*	0.00	0.00	0.00	0.00	874.40	26,855.75	0.00	0.00	0.00	874.40
MARTIN (23)*	0.00	0.00	0.00	0.00	0.00	0.00	0.00	0.00	145.62	145.62
NANSEMOND	0.00	0.00	0.00	0.00	0.00	0.00	0.00	0.00	422.99	422.99
OCCOQUAN BAY	0.00	0.00	0.00	0.00	0.00	0.00	0.00	0.00	642.07	642.07
PLUM TREE ISLAND	0.00	0.00	0.00	0.00	0.00	0.00	0.00	0.00	3,501.68	3,501.68
PRESQUILE	0.00	0.00	0.00	0.00	0.00	0.00	0.00	0.00	1,328.92	1,328.92
RAPPAHANNOCK RIVER	829.30	867,200.00	0.00	0.00	1,109.30	1,539,200.00	0.00	0.00	5,434.14	6,543.44
WALLOPS ISLAND	0.00	0.00	0.00	0.00	0.00	0.00	0.00	0.00	3,373.00	3,373.00
TOTAL 10	829.30	867,200.00	0.00	0.00	23,076.36	12,844,884.64	0.00	0.00	104,597.46	127,673.82

TABLE 1 - NATIONAL MIGRATORY BIRDS AREAS IN THE CONTERMINOUS UNITED STATES (continued)

	FISCAL YEAR MBCF ACQUISITION				CUMULATIVE TOTALS AT END OF FISCAL YEAR					
					MBCF					
	Purchased		Easement or Lease		Purchased		Easement or Lease		All Other	Total
State and Unit	Acres	Cost	Acres	Cost	Acres	Cost	Acres	Cost	Acres	Acres
WASHINGTON										
COLUMBIA	0.00	0.00	0.00	0.00	11,361.77	426,346.04	0.00	0.00	18,234.50	29,596.27
CONBOY LAKE	0.00	0.00	0.00	0.00	5,964.96	2,289,100.00	718.29	400,000.00	340.43	6,987.68
FSA INTEREST WA** *	0.00	0.00	0.00	0.00	0.00	0.00	0.00	0.00	965.92	965.92
LITTLE PEND OREILLE	0.00	0.00	0.00	0.00	4,216.65	27,414.00	0.00	0.00	38,376.92	42,593.57
MCNARY	0.00	0.00	0.00	0.00	185.16	865.00	0.00	0.00	15,320.23	15,505.39
NISQUALLY	0.00	0.00	0.00	0.00	2,494.56	3,861,990.17	0.55	3,000.00	1,437.18	3,932.29
PIERCE	0.00	0.00	0.00	0.00	0.00	0.00	0.00	0.00	329.38	329.38
RIDGEFIELD	0.00	0.00	0.00	0.00	4,670.16	4,033,600.00	1.74	21.00	545.80	5,217.70
SADDLE MOUNTAIN	0.00	0.00	0.00	0.00	0.00	0.00	0.00	0.00	161,485.93	161,485.93
SAN JUAN ISLANDS	0.00	0.00	0.00	0.00	0.00	0.00	0.00	0.00	448.53	448.53
STEIGERWALD LAKE	0.00	0.00	0.00	0.00	50.00	500,000.00	0.00	0.00	996.02	1,046.02
TOPPENISH	0.00	0.00	0.00	0.00	1,762.80	599,137.00	1.29	0.00	214.75	1,978.84
TURNBULL	80.00	152,000.00	0.00	0.00	13,909.32	507,411.38	0.00	0.00	2,702.75	16,612.07
UMATILLA (4) *	0.00	0.00	0.00	0.00	0.00	0.00	0.00	0.00	14,875.83	14,875.83
WILLAPA	0.00	0.00	0.00	0.00	8,616.42	5,122,010.74	0.12	0.00	7,303.80	15,920.34
TOTAL 13	80.00	152,000.00	0.00	0.00	53,231.80	17,367,874.33	721.99	403,021.00	262,541.97	317,495.76
WEST VIRGINIA										
FSA INTEREST WV ***	0.00	0.00	0.00	0.00	0.00	0.00	0.00	0.00	8.37	8.37
TOTAL 0	0.00	0.00	0.00	0.00	0.00	0.00	0.00	0.00	8.37	8.37
WISCONSIN										
FSA INTEREST WI ***	0.00	0.00	0.00	0.00	0.00	0.00	0.00	0.00	920.00	920.00
HORICON	0.00	0.00	0.00	0.00	21,098.37	555,237.42	29.00	356.00	277.95	21,405.32
NECEDAH	0.00	0.00	0.00	0.00	244.92	3,194.26	0.00	0.00	43,450.94	43,695.86
TREMPEALEAU	0.00	0.00	0.00	0.00	0.00	0.00	0.00	0.00	6,198.83	6,198.83
TOTAL 3	0.00	0.00	0.00	0.00	21,343.29	558,431.68	29.00	356.00	50,847.72	72,220.01
WYOMING										
BAMFORTH	0.00	0.00	0.00	0.00	964.80	6,368.00	0.00	0.00	201.23	1,166.03
COKEVILLE MEADOWS	0.00	0.00	0.00	3,881.34	4,738.89	2,101,412.61	320.00	11,905.21	4,200.43	9,259.32
FSA INTEREST WY ***	0.00	0.00	0.00	0.00	0.00	0.00	0.00	0.00	3,132.75	3,132.75
HUTTON LAKE	0.00	0.00	0.00	0.00	1,274.69	7,943.00	0.00	0.00	693.65	1,968.34
PATHFINDER	0.00	0.00	0.00	0.00	0.00	0.00	0.00	0.00	16,806.90	16,806.90
SEEDSKADEE	0.00	0.00	0.00	0.00	0.00	0.00	0.00	0.00	27,230.22	27,230.22
TOTAL 5	0.00	0.00	0.00	3,881.34	6,978.38	2,115,723.61	320.00	11,905.21	52,265.18	59,563.56
GRAND TOTAL 357	7,773.27	12,411,722.81	1,687.45	2,494,301.70	2,286,675.26	479,734,341.57	124,826.69	68,344,278.52	7,306,197.24	9,717,699.19

(1) Also in GEORGIA
(2) " " CALIFORNIA
(3) " " ARIZONA
(4) " " OREGON
(5) " " ALABAMA
(6) " " FLORIDA
(7) " " SOUTH CAROLINA
(8) " " MISSOURI
(9) " " IOWA, MINNESOTA AND WISCONSIN
(10) " " NEBRASKA
(11) " " ILLINOIS
(12) " " TEXAS
(13) " " ILLINOIS, MINNESOTA AND WISCONSIN
(14) " " TENNESSEE
(15) " " NEVADA
(16) " " VIRGINIA
(17) " " NEW MEXICO
(18) " " ILLINOIS, IOWA AND WISCONSIN
(19) " " IOWA
(20) " " SOUTH DAKOTA
(21) " " IDAHO
(22) " " KENTUCKY
(23) " " MARYLAND
(24) " " NORTH CAROLINA
(25) " " ILLINOIS, IOWA AND MINNESOTA
(26) " " WASHINGTON
(27) " " MISSISSIPPI
(28) " " LOUISIANA
(34) " " WEST VIRGINIA AND KENTUCKY

(35) Also in PENNSYLVANIA AND KENTUCKY
(36) " " NEW HAMPSHIRE
(37) " " MAINE
(38) " " WEST VIRGINIA AND PENNSYLVANIA
(39) " " NEW YORK
(40) " " NEW JERSEY
(41) " " MASSACHUSETTS
(42) " " VERMONT

* COUNTED IN ANOTHER STATE
** DENOTES INTERESTS TRANSFERRED BY FARMERS HOME
ADMINISTRATION, DEPARTMENT OF AGRICULTURE

TABLE 2 - NATIONAL WATERFOWL PRODUCTION AREAS

	FISCAL YEAR MBCF ACQUISITION				CUMULATIVE TOTALS AT END OF FISCAL YEAR					
					MBCF					
	Purchased		Easement or Lease		Purchased		Easement or Lease		All Other	Total
State and Unit	Acres	Cost	Acres	Cost	Acres	Cost	Acres	Cost	Acres	Acres
IDAHO										
OXFORD SLOUGH	0.00	0.00	0.00	0.00	1,878.41	530,000.00	0.00	0.00	0.00	1,878.41
TOTAL 1	0.00	0.00	0.00	0.00	1,878.41	530,000.00	0.00	0.00	0.00	1,878.41
IOWA										
BOONE	0.00	0.00	0.00	0.00	391.33	599,600.00	0.00	0.00	0.00	391.33
BUENA VISTA	0.00	0.00	0.00	0.00	69.09	169,000.00	0.00	0.00	0.00	69.09
CERRO GORDO	226.00	452,000.00	0.00	0.00	2,720.25	3,284,677.82	5.70	10,200.00	0.00	2,725.95
CLAY	0.00	0.00	0.00	0.00	867.93	1,146,206.85	0.00	0.00	0.00	867.93
DICKINSON	306.30	605,240.00	0.00	0.00	4,567.43	5,635,756.00	98.00	37,725.00	635.34	5,300.77
EMMET	0.00	0.00	0.00	0.00	1,445.85	1,895,075.00	16.00	40,000.00	249.99	1,711.84
GREENE	0.00	0.00	0.00	0.00	669.05	1,260,700.00	0.00	0.00	0.00	669.05
GUTHRIE	0.00	0.00	0.00	0.00	185.53	293,840.00	0.00	0.00	0.00	185.53
HANCOCK	0.00	0.00	0.00	0.00	802.70	545,480.26	7.00	2,250.00	0.00	809.70
KOSSUTH	0.00	0.00	0.00	0.00	2,213.08	3,955,196.98	23.00	28,775.00	0.00	2,236.08
OSCEOLA	0.00	0.00	0.00	0.00	0.00	0.00	37.00	17,250.00	4.00	41.00
PALO ALTO	0.00	0.00	0.00	0.00	627.56	844,092.65	224.00	222,850.00	58.00	909.56
POCAHONTAS	155.40	357,400.00	0.00	0.00	379.16	812,400.00	0.00	0.00	0.00	379.16
POLK	0.00	0.00	0.00	0.00	110.00	241,500.00	0.00	0.00	0.00	110.00
SAC	192.90	543,000.00	0.00	0.00	489.42	906,880.00	0.00	0.00	0.00	489.42
WINNEBAGO	0.00	0.00	0.00	0.00	1,023.15	1,138,300.31	105.00	54,025.00	0.00	1,128.15
WORTH	0.00	0.00	0.00	0.00	1,491.84	1,088,329.87	18.00	9,250.00	0.00	1,509.84
WRIGHT	0.00	0.00	0.00	0.00	1,528.09	2,228,025.00	0.00	0.00	0.00	1,528.09
TOTAL 18	880.60	1,957,640.00	0.00	0.00	19,581.46	26,045,060.74	533.70	422,325.00	947.33	21,062.49
MAINE										
CARLTON POND	0.00	0.00	0.00	0.00	1,068.21	18,276.08	0.00	0.00	0.00	1,068.21
TOTAL 1	0.00	0.00	0.00	0.00	1,068.21	18,276.08	0.00	0.00	0.00	1,068.21
MICHIGAN										
JACKSON	0.00	0.00	0.00	0.00	160.00	170,000.00	0.00	0.00	0.00	160.00
VAN BUREN	0.00	0.00	0.00	0.00	77.08	43,600.00	0.00	0.00	0.00	77.08
TOTAL 2	0.00	0.00	0.00	0.00	237.08	213,600.00	0.00	0.00	0.00	237.08
MINNESOTA										
AITKIN	0.00	0.00	0.00	0.00	69.86	28,000.00	0.00	0.00	0.00	69.86
BECKER	0.00	0.00	0.00	0.00	12,346.74	3,733,020.56	2,012.14	533,335.10	53.22	14,412.10
BIG STONE	0.00	0.00	98.80	74,375.00	11,502.69	2,294,645.83	8,306.23	1,635,856.16	6.27	19,815.19
BLUE EARTH	0.00	0.00	0.00	0.00	1,148.61	1,598,250.00	78.70	141,575.00	58.48	1,285.79
CARVER	0.00	0.00	0.00	0.00	0.00	0.00	47.57	68,976.50	219.00	266.57
CASS	0.00	0.00	0.00	0.00	0.00	0.00	0.00	0.00	43.00	43.00
CHIPPEWA	0.00	0.00	0.00	0.00	244.10	127,050.00	57.00	32,900.00	0.00	301.10
CLAY	155.56	115,500.00	0.00	0.00	10,541.45	3,095,045.18	3,318.42	772,797.15	11.17	13,871.04
CLEARWATER	0.00	0.00	21.00	4,225.00	0.00	0.00	864.00	129,075.00	0.00	864.00
COTTONWOOD	151.32	245,400.00	0.00	0.00	3,096.46	1,625,453.85	192.31	107,375.00	0.00	3,289.31
DAKOTA	0.00	0.00	0.00	0.00	73.90	201,747.00	0.00	0.00	0.05	73.95
DOUGLAS	0.00	0.00	0.00	0.00	9,125.07	1,763,515.20	6,177.79	978,805.98	498.62	15,801.48
FARIBAULT	0.00	0.00	0.00	0.00	830.06	800,991.80	129.37	110,775.00	0.00	959.43
FREEBORN	0.00	0.00	0.00	0.00	1,631.99	1,833,367.25	143.26	145,625.00	134.93	1,910.18
GRANT	0.00	0.00	26.70	11,925.00	9,885.77	2,609,508.12	3,641.80	1,329,879.00	174.52	13,702.09
JACKSON	0.00	0.00	0.00	0.00	4,169.56	2,835,810.28	383.09	547,400.00	0.00	4,552.65
KANDIYOHI	0.00	0.00	0.00	0.00	13,561.17	5,611,962.93	4,264.83	562,451.80	1.68	17,827.68
LAC QUI PARLE	0.00	0.00	118.10	85,775.00	3,728.79	903,439.73	1,775.17	738,516.00	278.63	5,782.59
LESUEUR	0.00	0.00	0.00	0.00	350.91	438,754.50	209.15	126,728.50	62.88	622.94
LINCOLN	98.00	80,850.00	551.48	389,200.00	852.26	504,500.00	1,068.85	591,596.04	0.00	1,921.11
LYON	0.00	0.00	0.00	0.00	1,542.02	1,269,720.00	333.80	163,330.00	13.54	1,889.36
MAHNOMEN	0.00	0.00	24.00	3,225.00	5,399.33	853,558.90	4,971.00	164,736.00	0.00	10,370.33
MARTIN	0.00	0.00	0.00	0.00	70.89	45,369.60	271.65	287,184.39	0.00	342.54
MCLEOD	273.19	601,000.00	0.00	0.00	1,224.85	1,737,793.00	739.27	456,944.90	0.00	1,964.12
MEEKER	157.30	185,165.00	52.97	48,025.00	4,866.29	4,157,389.10	2,311.11	976,767.00	0.00	7,177.40
MURRAY	0.00	0.00	0.00	0.00	2,158.05	2,601,977.00	21.00	44,300.00	0.00	2,179.05
NOBLES	0.00	0.00	0.00	0.00	442.94	580,802.00	26.00	15,600.00	78.71	547.65
NORMAN	0.00	0.00	0.00	0.00	1,120.00	400,000.00	0.00	0.00	0.00	1,120.00
OTTER TAIL	0.00	0.00	80.77	45,050.00	20,760.80	6,879,052.26	14,126.20	3,082,305.25	145.87	35,032.87
POLK	0.00	0.00	0.00	0.00	12,441.29	2,540,752.86	1,743.80	263,925.00	0.00	14,185.09

TABLE 2 - NATIONAL WATERFOWL PRODUCTION AREAS

| | FISCAL YEAR MBCF ACQUISITION | | | | CUMULATIVE TOTALS AT END OF FISCAL YEAR | | | | | |
| | Purchased | | Easement or Lease | | MBCF Purchased | | Easement or Lease | | All Other | Total |
State and Unit	Acres	Cost	Acres	Cost	Acres	Cost	Acres	Cost	Acres	Acres
MINNESOTA (continued)										
POPE	0.00	0.00	195.68	116,759.50	12,755.79	2,396,245.07	9,115.76	1,177,636.70	208.32	22,079.87
RENVILLE	0.00	0.00	0.00	0.00	1,453.03	1,840,340.00	0.00	0.00	0.00	1,453.03
RICE	0.00	0.00	0.00	0.00	315.60	438,999.35	473.74	721,441.25	96.50	885.84
ROCK	0.00	0.00	0.00	0.00	0.00	0.00	11.00	9,350.00	0.00	11.00
SCOTT	0.00	0.00	0.00	0.00	40.00	109,200.00	164.21	248,001.00	0.00	204.21
SIBLEY	0.00	0.00	0.00	0.00	793.52	1,007,681.32	253.25	173,190.00	112.36	1,159.13
STEARNS	63.65	215,980.00	0.00	0.00	9,133.36	2,926,713.87	1,542.71	670,636.70	233.00	10,909.07
STEELE	0.00	0.00	0.00	0.00	630.11	653,244.00	0.00	0.00	0.00	630.11
STEVENS	0.00	0.00	14.30	10,3500.00	9,515.66	3,463,001.64	1,220.30	348,965.00	72.22	10,808.18
SWIFT	0.00	0.00	0.00	0.00	7,601.12	1,804,930.17	1,865.87	700,969.40	0.00	9,466.99
TODD	0.00	0.00	0.00	0.00	802.85	385,672.20	16.00	7,680.00	0.00	818.85
TRAVERSE	0.00	0.00	0.00	0.00	4,105.55	1,469,588.63	1,443.61	307,665.00	0.00	5,549.16
WASECA	0.00	0.00	0.00	0.00	248.78	408,000.00	0.00	0.00	0.00	248.78
WATONWAN	0.00	0.00	0.00	0.00	56.65	31,157.50	168.42	112,209.80	0.00	225.07
WILKIN	0.00	0.00	0.00	0.00	2,433.26	900,064.35	309.00	93,750.00	0.00	2,742.26
WRIGHT	0.00	0.00	0.00	0.00	2,500.92	2,527,820.90	437.50	223,575.00	0.00	2,938.42
YELLOW MEDICINE	0.00	0.00	0.00	0.00	959.58	703,683.30	235.09	98,027.40	0.00	1,194.67
TOTAL 47	899.02	1,443,895.00	1,162.80	784,684.50	186,531.63	72,137,819.25	74,470.51	18,901,857.02	2,502.97	263,505.11
MONTANA										
BLAINE	0.00	0.00	0.00	0.00	2,435.26	167,340.00	2,972.20	240,350.00	0.00	5,407.46
CASCADE	0.00	0.00	0.00	0.00	727.46	299,606.00	78.00	15,550.00	0.00	805.46
CHOUTEAU	0.00	0.00	0.00	1,541.00	2,136.13	538,543.00	501.00	22,408.00	0.00	2,637.13
DANIELS	0.00	0.00	0.00	0.00	1,080.58	97,669.00	472.65	41,125.00	546.52	2,099.75
FLATHEAD	0.00	0.00	0.00	0.00	4,410.31	2,246,518.00	0.00	0.00	807.92	5,218.23
GLACIER	0.00	0.00	265.00	25,700.00	94.20	17,898.00	10,146.83	953,495.00	96.50	10,337.53
GOLDEN VALLEY	0.00	0.00	0.00	165.92	760.27	76,427.00	160.00	5,314.95	0.00	920.27
HILL	0.00	0.00	0.00	851.00	0.00	0.00	918.00	79,170.00	378.93	1,296.93
LAKE	0.00	0.00	0.00	0.00	1,480.86	1,460,555.00	4,146.05	3,103,430.00	1,820.14	7,447.05
LEWIS AND CLARK	0.00	0.00	0.00	0.00	0.00	0.00	1,525.50	424,100.00	320.00	1,845.50
LIBERTY	0.00	0.00	0.00	0.00	0.00	0.00	428.00	14,100.00	0.00	428.00
MUSSELSHELL	0.00	0.00	0.00	720.00	532.45	163,001.00	160.00	7,355.00	0.00	692.45
PETROLEUM	0.00	0.00	0.00	0.00	40.00	23,800.00	0.00	0.00	0.00	40.00
PHILLIPS *	0.00	0.00	805.42	30,545.04	6,877.83	1,371,863.00	24,419.47	1,635,681.95	1,372.50	32,669.80
PONDERA	0.00	0.00	0.00	0.00	640.00	93,000.00	8,487.01	1,760,000.00	0.00	9,127.01
POWELL	108.00	225,000.00	759.00	445,000.00	1,527.60	683,084.00	23,203.06	6,650,635.00	4,092.33	28,822.99
ROOSEVELT	0.00	0.00	0.00	0.00	179.20	14,000.00	7,402.42	392,500.00	0.00	7,581.62
SHERIDAN	0.00	0.00	0.00	0.00	9,328.01	950,442.23	9,703.70	679,255.00	1,710.13	20,761.84
STILLWATER	0.00	0.00	0.00	0.00	1,828.10	207,625.00	0.00	0.00	0.38	1,828.48
TETON *	0.00	0.00	0.00	0.00	1,486.05	376,253.00	4,964.42	78,500.00	136.04	6,586.51
TOOLE	0.00	0.00	0.00	0.00	4,329.18	983,964.00	12,161.09	916,245.00	5.28	16,495.55
VALLEY	0.00	0.00	0.00	0.00	0.00	0.00	201.00	28,160.00	0.00	201.00
YELLOWSTONE	0.00	0.00	0.00	0.00	486.42	55,600.00	0.00	0.00	0.00	486.42
TOTAL 23	108.00	225,000.00	1,829.42	504,522.96	40,661.21	9,847,188.23	112,050.40	17,049,927.90	11,306.67	164,018.22
NEBRASKA										
ADAMS	0.00	0.00	0.00	0.00	160.00	110,000.00	0.00	11,316.89	234.56	394.56
CLAY	0.00	0.00	0.00	0.00	4,216.27	1,622,444.00	0.00	0.00	2,148.31	6,364.58
FILLMORE	0.00	0.00	0.00	0.00	2,937.60	1,142,453.00	6.60	24.00	400.00	3,344.20
FRANKLIN	0.00	0.00	0.00	0.00	1,625.96	402,698.00	0.00	0.00	157.36	1,783.32
GOSPER	0.00	0.00	0.00	0.00	1,451.50	233,923.00	0.00	0.00	0.00	1,451.50
HALL *	0.00	0.00	0.00	0.00	328.77	433,000.00	0.00	0.00	320.70	649.47
HAMILTON *	0.00	0.00	0.00	0.00	400.00	407,450.00	0.00	5,899.02	726.00	1,126.00
KEARNEY *	0.00	0.00	0.00	0.00	2,874.43	657,681.00	0.00	0.00	175.50	3,049.93
PHELPS	0.00	0.00	0.00	0.00	4,195.14	3,052,111.00	0.00	0.00	400.00	4,595.14
POLK FSA ***	0.00	0.00	0.00	0.00	0.00	0.00	0.00	0.00	140.78	140.78
SALINE FSA ***	0.00	0.00	0.00	0.00	0.00	0.00	0.00	0.00	104.35	104.35
SEWARD	0.00	0.00	0.00	0.00	283.38	101,746.45	0.00	0.00	187.76	471.14
YORK *	0.00	0.00	0.00	0.00	679.20	194,429.00	0.00	0.00	241.00	920.20
TOTAL 11	0.00	0.00	0.00	0.00	19,152.25	8,357,935.45	6.60	17,239.91	5,236.32	24,395.17

TABLE 2 - NATIONAL WATERFOWL PRODUCTION AREAS (continued)

		FISCAL YEAR MBCF ACQUISITION				CUMULATIVE TOTALS AT END OF FISCAL YEAR					
						MBCF					
		Purchased		Easement or Lease		Purchased		Easement or Lease		All Other	Total
State and Unit		Acres	Cost	Acres	Cost	Acres	Cost	Acres	Cost	Acres	Acres
NORTH DAKOTA											
BARNES	*	0.00	0.00	46.00	19,050.00	6,661.68	958,087.00	17,342.00	789,785.00	2,066.00	26,069.68
BENSON	*	0.00	0.00	0.00	0.00	7,296.77	607,908.00	35,547.00	987,855.00	6,612.12	49,455.89
BOTTINEAU	*	0.00	0.00	44.00	11,025.00	2,334.06	200,763.00	29,036.48	1,333,355.00	872.57	32,243.11
BURKE		0.00	0.00	76.00	12,350.00	3,544.19	180,068.00	25,353.00	657,505.00	16,385.16	46,282.35
BURLEIGH	*	0.00	0.00	823.00	86,500.00	9,451.44	1,899,164.00	26,078.00	624,025.00	16,835.83	52,365.27
CASS		0.00	0.00	0.00	0.00	3,439.89	628,344.00	1,709.00	133,825.00	50.90	5,199.79
CAVALIER	*	0.00	0.00	0.00	0.00	10,129.12	1,354,471.00	13,550.00	250,540.00	1,083.71	24,762.83
DICKEY	*	0.00	0.00	608.00	271,425.00	9,735.40	1,150,816.00	26,812.80	1,186,200.00	12,228.29	48,776.49
DIVIDE		0.00	0.00	0.00	0.00	9,444.62	474,790.00	34,574.09	646,785.00	1,317.83	45,336.54
EDDY	*	0.00	0.00	0.00	0.00	4,627.21	498,001.00	11,810.63	314,995.00	446.34	16,884.18
EMMONS	*	0.00	0.00	0.00	0.00	3,135.29	174,321.75	11,492.00	262,750.00	788.60	15,415.89
FOSTER		0.00	0.00	0.00	0.00	1,487.07	96,568.00	6,828.00	200,465.00	0.00	8,315.07
GRAND FORKS		160.00	33,200.00	0.00	0.00	6,141.98	1,246,722.05	1,118.00	46,485.00	641.26	7,901.24
GRIGGS		0.00	0.00	0.00	0.00	3,069.46	373,990.00	16,677.00	536,830.00	259.25	20,005.71
HETTINGER		0.00	0.00	0.00	0.00	0.00	0.00	0.00	0.00	1,202.60	1,202.60
KIDDER	*	0.00	0.00	459.00	33,150.00	5,547.52	438,439.00	63,955.00	1,008,605.00	12,965.32	84,467.84
LA MOURE	*	0.00	0.00	0.00	0.00	4,799.96	505,095.00	13,121.40	509,949.00	1,590.19	19,511.55
LOGAN	*	0.00	0.00	167.00	9,700.00	11,226.24	1,006,598.00	37,257.60	780,786.00	7,364.48	55,848.32
MCHENRY	*	0.00	0.00	1,324.00	94,050.00	4,888.80	374,404.50	29,122.00	899,220.00	18,488.50	52,499.30
MCINTOSH	*	0.00	0.00	0.00	0.00	17,373.48	1,368,865.00	29,761.00	709,000.00	570.08	47,704.56
MCLEAN		0.00	0.00	120.00	17,150.00	4,068.29	420,234.00	22,294.00	1,404,440.00	16,306.60	42,668.89
MOUNTRAIL	*	0.00	0.00	301.00	24,225.00	9,905.10	940,661.00	31,178.00	907,980.00	23,275.72	64,358.82
NELSON	*	0.00	0.00	0.00	0.00	3,203.23	174,341.00	37,886.70	1,336,445.00	803.91	41,863.84
PEMBINA	*	0.00	0.00	0.00	0.00	2,258.56	218,677.00	139.00	1,900.00	293.90	2,691.46
PIERCE	*	0.00	0.00	0.00	0.00	8,396.26	922,055.00	36,246.00	1,162,285.00	9,727.85	54,370.11
RAMSEY	*	0.00	0.00	0.00	0.00	8,183.04	1,144,252.00	28,730.00	821,835.00	1,679.49	38,592.53
RANSOM		0.00	0.00	0.00	0.00	4,315.02	617,357.00	20,271.60	1,475,525.00	3,533.88	28,120.50
RENVILLE		0.00	0.00	135.00	41,400.00	311.09	23,523.00	15,571.00	1,418,715.00	31.60	15,913.69
RICHLAND		0.00	0.00	0.00	0.00	5,992.25	938,052.00	1,946.80	351,595.00	4,104.60	12,043.65
ROLETTE		0.00	0.00	0.00	0.00	5,694.03	759,347.00	19,893.01	429,420.00	722.96	26,310.00
SARGENT	*	0.00	0.00	0.00	0.00	3,537.46	305,439.00	14,203.00	846,035.00	7,207.79	24,948.25
SHERIDAN	*	0.00	0.00	0.00	0.00	7,661.50	468,427.00	31,427.59	1,103,970.00	16,416.12	55,505.21
STEELE		0.00	0.00	0.00	0.00	3,249.25	538,345.00	4,045.00	274,320.00	359.30	7,653.55
STUTSMAN	*	0.00	0.00	356.29	17,000.00	23,401.84	1,308,016.00	41,925.99	978,615.00	17,993.38	83,321.21
TOWNER	*	0.00	0.00	24.00	725.00	3,837.02	494,146.00	24,286.00	484,715.00	5,946.31	34,069.33
TRAILL		0.00	0.00	0.00	0.00	719.25	75,109.00	234.00	4,830.00	0.00	953.25
WALSH	*	0.00	0.00	0.00	0.00	1,393.19	98,128.00	8,738.40	118,801.00	751.23	10,882.82
WARD		0.00	0.00	0.00	0.00	5,868.60	489,211.00	37,861.61	1,411,639.00	7,070.10	51,800.31
WELLS	*	0.00	0.00	0.00	0.00	7,471.61	1,153,059.00	13,318.00	616,277.00	3,473.62	24,263.23
WILLIAMS	*	0.00	0.00	0.00	0.00	4,163.17	278,057.00	8,298.00	214,100.00	606.00	13,067.17
TOTAL	40	160.00	33,200.00	4,483.29	636,750.00	237,963.94	24,903,851.30	831,608.70	27,242,401.00	222,073.39	1,291,646.03
SOUTH DAKOTA											
AURORA	*	0.00	0.00	1,194.00	285,140.00	4,716.08	622,316.00	33,941.62	4,062,945.00	495.90	39,153.60
BEADLE	*	0.00	0.00	5,020.94	1,492,525.00	7,256.45	1,651,212.69	39,348.99	5,046,795	1,665.89	48,271.33
BON HOMME	*	0.00	0.00	0.00	0.00	1,174.17	323,624.90	159.00	4,305.00	93.73	1,426.90
BROOKINGS	*	0.00	0.00	0.00	0.00	6,051.85	1,430,276.70	7,126.48	1,618,016.00	1,235.50	14,413.83
BROWN		0.00	0.00	1,061.56	356,850.00	4,094.93	819,223.80	48,990.46	6,315,000.00	1,439.39	54,524.78
BRULE		0.00	0.00	301.00	75,565.00	1,074.13	89,404.00	17,982.26	1,414,230.00	839.43	19,895.82
BUFFALO		0.00	0.00	0.00	0.00	0.00	0.00	1,343.61	48,000.00	916.52	2,260.13
CAMPBELL		0.00	0.00	0.00	0.00	1,919.71	185,541.00	22,197.15	1,554,480.00	395.00	24,511.86
CHARLES MIX	*	0.00	0.00	255.48	44,475.00	4,098.15	1,142,147.00	5,959.63	397,425.00	1,167.81	11,225.59
CLARK	*	0.00	0.00	160.00	39,300.00	5,873.11	814,503.90	44,455.03	2,606,175.00	1,013.23	51,341.37
CLAY	*	0.00	0.00	0.00	0.00	40.00	8,000.00	7.00	200.00	52.50	99.50
CODINGTON	*	0.00	0.00	0.00	0.00	5,089.31	882,837.70	9,993.03	653,065.00	1,456.65	16,538.99
CORSON FSA	***	0.00	0.00	0.00	0.00	0.00	0.00	0.00	0.00	1,105.90	1,105.90
DAVISON	*	0.00	0.00	0.00	0.00	229.92	24,540.00	179.00	14,365.00	175.10	584.02
DAY		0.00	0.00	562.62	126,900.00	6,332.63	457,107.00	44,039.00	2,987,470.00	1,647.75	52,019.38
DEUEL	*	0.00	0.00	137.33	38,200.00	3,186.37	459,022.00	22,462.88	1,849,200.00	1,958.89	27,608.14
DEWEY FSA	***	0.00	0.00	0.00	0.00	0.00	0.00	0.00	0.00	956.80	956.80
DOUGLAS	*	0.00	0.00	441.79	108,710.00	3,852.05	647,691.00	3,628.96	290,675.00	713.17	8,194.18
EDMUNDS	*	0.00	0.00	2,327.97	337,900.00	8,965.76	1,717,201.00	117,247.89	8,250,510.00	983.80	127,197.45
FAULK	*	0.00	0.00	1,551.81	248,420.00	2,566.88	480,995.00	127,850.80	7,876,575.00	1,442.40	131,860.08
GRANT		0.00	0.00	229.72	46,620.00	5,362.99	1,005,000.00	16,151.66	1,009,460.00	0.00	21,514.65

47

TABLE 2 - NATIONAL WATERFOWL PRODUCTION AREAS (continued)

State and Unit		FISCAL YEAR MBCF ACQUISITION Purchased Acres	Purchased Cost	Easement or Lease Acres	Easement or Lease Cost	CUMULATIVE TOTALS AT END OF FISCAL YEAR MBCF Purchased Acres	Purchased Cost	Easement or Lease Acres	Easement or Lease Cost	All Other Acres	Total Acres
SOUTH DAKOTA (continued)											
HAAKON FSA	** *	0.00	0.00	0.00	0.00	0.00	0.00	0.00	0.00	1,806.10	1,806.10
HAMLIN	*	0.00	0.00	0.00	0.00	3,375.89	943,938.00	6,020.24	1,006,305.00	323.90	9,720.03
HAND	*	0.00	0.00	2,687.67	576,950.00	3,671.31	580,260.35	50,893.29	4,064,625.00	1,890.30	56,401.50
HANSON	*	0.00	0.00	0.00	0.00	1,075.60	281,853.00	2,680.48	136,130.00	132.80	3,888.88
HUGHES		0.00	0.00	0.00	0.00	455.99	82,800.00	744.50	48,825.00	0.00	1,200.49
HUTCHINSON	*	0.00	0.00	44.00	25,3500.00	789.51	227,646.25	1,057.00	151,075.00	172.50	2,019.01
HYDE	*	0.00	0.00	3,140.02	504,635.00	0.00	0.00	29,487.18	2,429,730.00	6,969.11	36,456.29
JERAULD	*	0.00	0.00	1,653.78	443,475.00	1,430.40	217,041.00	22,409.71	2,105,965.00	725.40	24,565.51
JONES FSA	** *	0.00	0.00	0.00	0.00	0.00	0.00	0.00	0.00	232.00	232.00
KINGSBURY	*	0.00	0.00	536.41	252,525.00	5,256.36	1,258,255.50	23,259.00	2,389,828.00	2,751.87	31,267.23
LAKE	*	1.98	2,000.00	0.00	0.00	5,667.07	1,281,607.75	6,432.32	1,712,710.00	911.24	13,010.63
LINCOLN		0.00	0.00	0.00	0.00	177.22	39,925.00	300.50	112,645.00	0.00	477.72
MARSHALL	*	0.00	0.00	360.01	99,750.00	10,098.51	1,923,929.00	56,098.14	3,797,356.00	963.90	67,160.55
MCCOOK		0.00	0.00	0.00	0.00	3,362.96	680,845.60	6,316.50	899,970.00	835.37	10,514.83
MCPHERSON	*	0.00	0.00	2,440.85	317,150.00	19,254.66	3,373,536.80	134,067.91	6,837,540.00	9,345.44	162,668.01
MINER	*	8.83	2,655.00	2,516.55	1,341.275.00	1,545.87	153,695.00	20,790.67	3,956,665.00	1,299.80	23,636.34
MINNEHAHA	*	0.00	0.00	0.00	0.00	4,499.63	1,100,286.00	1,640.96	351,295.00	10.00	6,150.59
MOODY	*	0.00	0.00	0.00	0.00	2,903.78	927,478.85	1,959.02	645,930.00	705.89	5,568.69
POTTER	*	0.00	0.00	0.00	0.00	652.63	71,179.00	23,258.73	1,324,755.00	415.10	24,326.46
ROBERTS	*	0.00	0.00	195.00	36,550.00	5,032.73	625,710.80	48,508.87	2,792,350.00	2,489.61	56,031.21
SANBORN	*	0.00	0.00	979.82	500,775.00	93.00	5,250.00	36,844.17	3,504,795.00	535.40	37,472.57
SPINK	*	0.00	0.00	700.54	146,400.00	2,226.43	388,680.00	26,129.64	2,893,200.00	1,042.90	29,398.97
STANLEY FSA	** *	0.00	0.00	0.00	0.00	0.00	0.00	0.00	0.00	1,404.80	1,404.80
SULLY	*	0.00	0.00	0.00	0.00	266.48	9,993.00	3,474.81	384,840.00	334.70	4,075.99
TRIPP FSA	** *	0.00	0.00	0.00	0.00	0.00	0.00	0.00	0.00	5.90	5.90
TURNER	*	0.00	0.00	0.00	0.00	850.09	430,044.90	353.00	106,090.00	126.90	1,329.99
UNION		0.00	0.00	0.00	0.00	96.02	22,331.00	0.00	0.00	0.00	96.02
WALWORTH	*	0.00	0.00	840.20	126,300.00	1,524.54	191,800.00	18,571.32	1,389,915.00	553.30	20,649.16
YANKTON		0.00	0.00	0.00	0.00	294.63	128,562.00	123.00	5,375.00	223.50	641.13
TOTAL	44	23.48	24,593.59	29,593.59	7,778,740.00	146,498.47	27,729,392.49	1,085,481.57	89,407,690.00	55,963.09	1,287,943.13
WISCONSIN											
ADAMS		0.00	0.00	0.00	0.00	344.00	172,500.00	0.00	0.00	0.00	344.00
COLUMBIA		253.24	464,750.00	0.00	0.00	3,227.88	2,959,816.45	0.00	0.00	0.00	3,227.88
DANE		0.00	0.00	0.00	0.00	1,535.58	1,984,875.65	0.00	0.00	55.50	1,591.08
DODGE		0.00	0.00	0.00	0.00	579.20	647,371.16	0.43	1,000.00	109.81	689.44
DUNN		0.00	0.00	0.00	0.00	438.68	502,200.00	0.00	0.00	183.30	621.98
FOND DU LAC		0.00	0.00	0.00	0.00	664.52	849,548.00	0.00	0.00	284.84	949.36
JEFFERSON		0.00	0.00	0.00	0.00	249.79	241,239.00	0.00	0.00	0.00	249.79
MANITOWOC		0.00	0.00	0.00	0.00	120.00	88,000.00	0.00	0.00	0.00	120.00
MARQUETTE		0.00	0.00	0.00	0.00	259.97	119,480.00	0.00	0.00	0.00	259.97
OZAUKEE		0.00	0.00	0.00	0.00	536.30	679,413.40	0.00	0.00	0.00	536.30
POLK		0.00	0.00	0.00	0.00	845.09	417,424.00	0.00	0.00	199.98	1,045.07
ROCK		0.00	0.00	0.00	0.00	349.32	302,358.71	0.00	0.00	0.00	349.32
SHEBOYGAN		0.00	0.00	0.00	0.00	485.92	1,322,636.94	0.00	0.00	223.99	709.91
ST. CROIX		0.00	0.00	0.00	0.00	4,857.17	4,995,404.56	0.64	1,500.00	235.73	5,093.54
WAUSHARA		0.00	0.00	0.00	0.00	232.30	243,000.00	0.00	6,000.00	0.00	232.30
WINNEBAGO		0.00	0.00	0.00	0.00	1,842.33	1,272,300.00	0.00	0.00	75.94	1,918.27
TOTAL	16	253.24	464,750.00	0.00	0.00	16,568.05	16,797,567.87	1.07	8,500.00	1,369.09	17,938.21
GRAND TOTAL	203	2,324.34	4,149,140.00	37,069.10	9,704,697.46	670,140.71	186,580,691.41	2,104,152.55	153,049,940.83	299,398.86	3,073,692.12

* THESE COUNTIES INCLUDE INTEREST TRANSFERRED BY FARMERS HOME ADMINISTRATION, DEPARTMENT OF AGRICULTURE

** DENOTES INTERESTS TRANSFERRED BY FARMERS HOME ADMINISTRATION, DEPARTMENT OF AGRICULTURE

North American Wetlands Conservation Fund (Summary) Fiscal Year 2004

The Migratory Bird Conservation Commission approved 82 standard wetland conservation project proposals for funding in Fiscal Year 2004 under the North American Wetlands Conservation Act. A total of $58,398,533 from the North American Wetlands Conservation Fund (Fund), together with $205,515,162 in partner funds, are supporting 39 projects in the United States, 31 in Canada, and 12 in Mexico. The following tables provide summary and detailed allocation information.

Fiscal Year 2004
Projects Approved by the Migratory Bird Conservation Commission and Active Under the North American Wetlands Conservation Act

Country	Number of Projects	Act Funds	Partner Funds	Acres Affected
U.S.	39	$34,762,725	$172,284,207	478,099
Canada	31	$21,219,897	$29,649,458	1,197,296
Mexico	12	$2,415,911	$3,581,499	212,267
Total	82	$58,398,533	$205,515,162	1,887,662

Additionally, 43 small grants were approved, totaling $1,956,709 from the Fund, supported by $11,413,813 in partner funds and affecting 12,022 acres.

United States Wetlands Conservation Standard Grant Proposals Approved by the Migratory Bird Conservation Commission For Fiscal Year 2004

Table Three

Project Name	State	NAWCA Grant ($)	Non-Fed Match	Non-Fed Non-Match	Federal Non-Match	Total Partners	Total Cost	Total Acres	MBCC Approval
Ace Basin: Edisto River Corridor									
Protection Project	SC	1,000,000	2,684,747	2,250	5,836,000	8,522,997	9,522,997	11,162	9/10/2003
Austin's Woods II	TX	480,000	555,411	148,500	30,000	733,911	1,213,911	1,046	9/10/2003
Avoca Island Restoration	LA	635,460	1,721,143	0	240,000	2,380,380	3,380,380	9,645	9/10/2003
Beaverhead Wetland Protection Project III	MT	1,000,000	2,140,380	0	240,000	2,380,380	3,380,380	7,876	3/3/2004
Channeled Scablands Focus Area II	WA	1,000,000	2,026,510	798,034	396,413	3,220,957	4,220,957	3,034	3/3/2004
Chenier Plain Coastal Wetlands Conservation I-									
White Lake Preserve	LA	334,000	1,060,508	0	11,168	1,071,676	1,405,676	71,130	3/3/2004
Devils Lake Drift Prairie Project III	ND	922,399	915,967	76,281	16,400	1,008,648	1,931,047	22,461	9/10/2003
Drift Prairie Wetland Project IV	ND	596,058	599,716	0	30,400	630,116	1,226,174	14,845	9/10/2003
Emiquon National Wildlife Refuge									
Partnership Project II	IL	1,000,000	2,034,400	0	1,477,000	3,511,400	4,511,400	2,925	3/3/2004
Glaciated Valleys of Northwest Montana	MT	929,952	1,918,081	322,075	3,218,850	5,459,006	6,388,958	3,352	3/3/2004
Grand River Watershed Project	MI	1,000,000	3,699,534	0	50,000	3,749,534	4,749,534	1,807	9/10/2003
Grassland Ecological Area III	CA	1,000,000	2,024,606	0	95,782	2,120,388	3,120,388	17,271	9/10/2003
Grasslands V- San Luis NWR Complex	CA	980,627	3,447,344	1,500	1,148,098	4,596,942	5,577,569	4,839	3/3/2004
Great Bay Estuary V									
(Lamprey - Piscassic Watershed)	NH	1,000,000	2,460,012	1,000	1,000	2,462,012	3,462,012	2,722	9/10/2003
Heart of the Pines Barrens	NJ	1,000,000	14,541,668	8,826,332	0	23,368,000	24,368,000	9,400	3/3/2004
Hickory Mound Impoundment Enhancement	FL	391,249	686,065	0	100,000	786,065	1,177,314	1,834	9/10/2003
Honey Lake Valley & Big									
Valley Wetlands Project	CA	852,828	1,806,652	10,000	367,336	2,183,988	3,036,816	5,723	9/10/2003
Horicon Marsh Headwaters	WI	683,142	1,366,285	0	0	1,366,285	2,049,427	1,868	9/10/2003
James River Lowlands/									
Missouri Coteau Project	SD	1,000,000	1,417,107	151,817	0	1,568,924	2,568,924	9,802	9/10/2003
Lewis & Clark Floodplain Heritage									
Partnership II	MO	1,000,000	2,254,506	1,200	18,863,251	21,118,957	22,118,957	15,341	9/10/2003
Lower Cohansey River Watershed	NJ	1,000,000	4,342,540	503,414	0	4,845,954	5,845,954	2,060	9/10/2003
Lower Obion River II	TN	1,000,000	2,916,109	0	0	2,916,109	3,916,109	1,897	3/3/2004
Malheur Lake Basin Project	OR	1,000,000	1,521,694	151,483	187,850	1,861,027	2,861,027	14,598	9/10/2003
Mobile - Tensaw Delta IV	AL	1,000,000	3,360,000	50,000	0	3,410,000	4,410,000	9,522	9/10/2003
North Carolina Onslow Bight Partnership	NC	1,000,000	2,941,000	2,500,000	15,000	5,456,000	6,456,000	13,867	3/3/2004
North Platte Basin Project I	NE	855,000	1,710,851	300,000	39,470	2,050,321	2,905,321	3,092	3/3/2004
North Sacramento Valley Wetland									
Habitat Project I	CA	1,000,000	2,107,453	0	5,652,559	7,760,012	8,760,012	10,503	9/10/2003
North San Joaquin Valley Wetland									
Habitat Project	CA	1,000,000	2,385,209	0	0	2,385,209	3,385,209	36,616	3/3/2004
Northern Tallgrass Prairie Wetland									
Conservation Initiative III	MN	1,000,000	2,149,352	0	19,021,919	21,171,271	22,171,271	26,594	9/10/2003
Oyster Bayou Restoration	LA	990,495	2,817,529	0	11,168	2,828,697	3,819,192	21,633	9/10/2003
Penholoway Swamp	GA	1,000,000	1,737,070	13,400	0	1,750,470	2,750,470	2,394	9/10/2003
Rainwater Basin Habitat Conservation Project	NE	1,000,000	1,252,606	30,325	102,755	1,385,686	2,385,686	6,119	3/3/2004
San Joaquin River I	CA	998,205	2,733,853	5,500	502,333	3,241,686	4,239,891	2,759	9/10/2003
Skagit/Samish Wetlands III	WA	1,000,000	2,006,310	759,591	104,981	2,870,882	3,870,882	1,022	3/3/2004
South Dakota Prairie Coteau Project	SD	860,000	1,371,813	0	6,438,616	7,810,429	8,670,429	91,865	3/3/2004
Texas Mid-Coast Wetlands Restoration	TX	893,310	1,790,399	0	571,026	2,361,425	3,254,735	7,472	3/3/2004
Torry, Kreamer Islands Restoration I	FL	400,000	820,000	750,500	0	1,570,500	1,970,500	3,005	9/10/2003
Upper Williamette Wetlands Conservation									
Initiative	OR	960,000	1,920,191	25,000	240,475	2,185,666	3,145,666	1,823	3/3/2004
Wisconsin Northwest Pothole Habitat Init IV	WI	1,000,000	2,614,366	80,000	136,000	2,830,366	3,830,366	3,155	3/3/2004
Number of Projects: 39		34,762,725	91,858,987	15,508,202	64,917,018	172,284,207	207,046,932	478,099	

United States Wetlands Conservation Small Grant Proposals Approved by the Migratory Bird Conservation Commission For Fiscal Year 2004

Table Three

Project Name	State	NAWCA Grant ($)	Non-Fed Match	Non-Fed Non-Match	Federal Non-Match	Total Partners	Total Cost	Total Acres	MBCC Approval
Akeley Swamp State Game Lands #282									
Hydrology Restoration	PA	50,000	100,000	0	25,000	125,000	175,000	168	9/10/2003
Alder Creek Farm	OR	50,000	150,752	0	70,000	220,752	270,752	50	9/10/2003
Bear Island Club, Inc. Enhancement Project	SC	49,750	142,735	0	0	142,735	192,485	500	9/10/2003
Buffalo Ridge Nesting Habitat									
Enhancement Project	MN	50,000	50,705	0	0	50,705	100,705	203	9/10/2003
Carney Island & the Causeway Intertidal Basin	ME	50,000	96,400	30,000	30,000	156,400	206,400	17	9/10/2003
Chautauqua Lake Outlet Greenway Project	NY	45,000	47,720	0	0	47,720	92,720	77	9/10/2003
Conserving Wetlands in the Beluga Wetlands									
Complex & Anchor River	AK	50,000	52,000	0	0	52,000	102,000	33	9/10/2003
Day's Marsh Acquisition	ME	50,000	73,300	0	0	73,300	123,300	68	9/10/2003
Delaware Habitat Stewardship Project	DE	50,000	100,000	0	0	100,000	150,000	35	9/10/2003
Double O Wetland Enhancement Project	SC	50,000	102,943	0	0	102,943	152,943	466	9/10/2003
Foster-Mattern Partnership Playas &									
Moist Soil Management	TX	16,250	19,559	0	0	019,559	35,809	89	9/10/2003
Fox River NWR Wetland Restoration	WI	17,500	17,500	5,000	0	22,500	40,000	100	9/10/2003
Gene Howe Wildlife Managment Area	TX	50,000	63,900	0	0	63,900	113,900	600	9/10/2003
Hutchinson Property on Lake Leelanau Narrows	MI	30,500	212,500	0	0	0212,500	243,000	43	9/10/2003
Island Center Marsh Acquisition	WA	50,000	430,000	0	0	430,000	480,000	30	9/10/2003
Killick Pond Conservation Area - Gannett Tract	ME	50,000	270,000	0	0	270,000	320,000	107	9/10/2003
Lea Lake Principal Spillway Construction	WI	50,000	120,00	0	5,000	125,000	175,000	230	9/10/2003
Liberty Marsh Restoration Project	NJ	32,000	34,836	0	86,000	120,836	152,836	207	9/10/2003
Limberlost & Loblolly Wetland Restoration Project	IN	48,000	96,084	0	0	96,084	144,084	113	9/10/2003
Little Tennessee River Riparian Restoration									
& Protection Project	NC	50,000	223,575	0	0	223,575	273,575	28	9/10/2003
Mohawk Pool Wetland Enhancement Project	NY	33,950	33,950	0	1,202,500	1,236,450	1,270,400	1,120	9/10/2003
Mud Lake WMA Project	MN	50,000	58,900	0	0	58,900	108,900	71	9/10/2003
Northeast Ohio Coastal Wetland & Native									
Grassland Project	OH	50,000	1,275,026	0	0	1,275,026	1,325,026	877	9/10/2003
Ormond Beach Bird Habitat Restoration Project	CA	35,000	38,546	0	0	38,546	73,546	100	9/10/2003
Pheasant Branch Conservancy Habitat									
Enhancement Project	WI	50,000	188,691	0	22,000	210,691	260,691	150	9/10/2003
Pigeon River Protection Project - Busch Acquisition	MI	50,000	1,200,000	250,000	0	1,450,000	1,500,000	200	9/10/2003
Pole Mountain Ranch Conservation Easement	CO	50,000	210,000	600,000	0	810,000	860,000	120	9/10/2003
Rainey Acres Farm Managed Wetlands									
Enhancement Project	SC	39,400	120,000	0	0	120,000	159,400	240	9/10/2003
Restoration of Myrtle Pond-Little St. Simons Islands	GA	42,000	50,000	0	0	50,000	92,000	95	9/10/2003
Restoration of the Latas Valley	PR	50,000	183,500	0	170,400	353,900	403,900	350	9/10/2003
Restoration of Wetlands for Wildlife at Spunky									
Bottoms Merwin Preserve	IL	49,993	58,570	0	0	58,570	108,563	265	9/10/2003
Riparian Corridor Restoration Along the									
Canadian River	TX	50,000	50,000	24,167	0	74,167	124,167	1,380	9/10/2003
Rose Lake Acquisition	WI	50,000	402,000	0	232,000	634,000	684,000	206	9/10/2003
Sares Bluff Conservation Project, Fidalgo Island	WA	50,000	1,050,000	0	0	1,050,000	1,100,000	37	9/10/2003
Sink Hole Marsh Enhancement Project	NY	45,000	57,500	0	0	57,500	102,500	1,200	9/10/2003
Skidmore Slough Estuarine Wetlands									
Conservation Project	WA	50,000	92,320	0	0	92,320	142,320	11	9/10/2003
Snatch Creek Acquisition Project	SD	50,000	170,247	0	0	170,247	220,247	240	9/10/2003
Stikine River Wetlands Acquisition:									
North Knig Slough (Schwartz Tract)	AK	50,000	219,000	0	245,000	464,000	514,000	160	9/10/2003
Turkey Run Wildlife Area Wetland Development -									
Des Moines River	IA	50,000	65,000	198,000	0	263,000	313,000	232	9/10/2003
Upper Delaware Wetland Resoration Project	PA	50,000	150,000	0	0	150,000	200,000	80	9/10/2003
Wildlife Habitat Enhancement at Lake Alice WMA	NY	46,902	61,473	0	0	61,473	108,375	1,388	9/10/2003
Yahara River - Cherokee Marsh Wetland Restoration	WI	25,464	25,464	0	0	25,464	50,928	280	9/10/2003
Yaquina Estuary Acquisition	OR	50,000	54,050	0	0	54,050	104,050	62	9/10/2003
Number of Projects: 43		**1,956,709**	**8,218,746**	**1,107,167**	**2,087,900**	**11,413,813**	**13,370,522**	**12,022**	

Canadian Wetlands Conservation Proposals Approved by the Migratory Bird Conservation Commission For Fiscal Year 2004

Table Four

Project Name	Province	NAWCA Grant ($)	Non-Fed $ Match	Non-Fed Non-Match $	Total Partners	Total $ Cost	Total Acres	MBCC Approval
Acadian Peninsula of New Brunswick &								
New Brunswick & the SW Coast of Newfoundland	NB, NF	124,640	124,640	53,200	177,840	302,480	450	6/9/2004
Alberta - Critical Wetland & Upland Habitat	AB	407,360	407,360	271,635	678,995	1,086,355	6,090	6/9/2004
Alberta Habitat Program	AB	3,968,340	3,968,340	914,280	4,882,620	8,850,960	33,697	6/9/2004
Alberta Habitat Program	AB, BC	1,729,728	1,729,728	375,200	2,104,928	3,834,656	14,787	9/10/2003
Conservation of Critical Wetlands & Assoc.								
Upland Habitats, Coastal British Columbia	BC	336,960	336,960	402,000	738,960	1,075,920	390	9/10/2003
Conservation of Critical Wetlands & Assoc. Upland Habitats	BC	925,058	925,058	608,000	1,533,058	2,458,116	1,140	6/9/2004
Great Lakes Wetland Habitat Project	ON	250,800	250,800	247,000	497,800	748,600	400	6/9/2004
Internationally Important Coastal & Interior Wetland Habitats	AB, BC	609,302	609,302	1,474,400	2,083,702	2,693,004	1,700	6/9/2004
Manitoba Critical Wetland & Upland Habitat	MB	76,000	76,000	57,000	133,000	209,000	1,500	6/9/2004
Manitoba Prairie Parkland Program	MB	864,864	864,864	33,500	898,364	1,763,228	12,099	9/10/2003
Manitoba Prairie Parkland Program	MB	1,771,560	1,771,560	135,280	1,906,840	3,678,400	29,582	6/9/2004
New Brunswick Wetlands Conservation	NB	95,810	95,810	3,350	99,160	194,970	249	9/10/2003
New Brunswick Wetlands Conservation	NB	218,880	218,880	11,400	230,280	449,160	1,735	6/9/2004
Newfoundland & Labrador Coastal & Inland Freshwater Wetlands	NF	28,475	28,475	6,700	35,175	63,650	700	9/10/2003
Newfoundland & Labrador Coastal & Inland Freshwater Wetlands	NF	65,360	65,360	7,600	72,960	138,320	275	6/9/2004
Nova Scotia Coastal & Inland Wetlands	NS	67,000	67,000	6,700	73,700	140,700	173	9/10/2003
Nova Scotia Coastal & Inland Wetlands	NS	164,920	164,920	9,120	174,040	338,960	349	6/9/2004
Ontario Project	ON	1,095,160	1,095,160	357,200	1,452,360	2,547,520	3,725	6/9/2004
Ontario Regional Project	ON	343,040	343,040	67,000	410,040	753,080	637	9/10/2003
Ontario Wetland Habitat Fund Program	ON	76,000	76,000	171,000	247,000	323,000	2,000	6/9/2004
Ontario Wetland Habitat Fund Program	ON	134,000	134,000	399,320	533,320	667,320	5,000	9/10/2003
Prince Edward Island Wetlands in the Agricultural Landscape	PE	47,570	47,570	13,400	60,970	108,540	952	9/10/2003
Prince Edward Island Wetlands in the Agricultural Landscape	PE	109,440	109,440	7,600	117,040	226,480	390	6/9/2004
Quebec - Protecting Wetland & Upland Habitat	QC	148,200	148,200	660,626	808,826	957,026	1,647	6/9/2004
Quebec / St. Lawrence Watershed	QC	547,960	547,960	437,000	984,960	1,532,920	2,068	6/9/2004
Quebec / St. Lawrence, Abitibi Lowlands, & Boreal Forest	QC	238,520	238,520	318,250	556,770	795,290	1,023	9/10/2003
Saskatchewan Habitat Program	SK	1,640,953	1,640,953	120,600	1,761,553	3,402,506	17,827	9/10/2003
Saskatchewan Habitat Program	SK	3,968,340	3,968,340	437,000	4,405,340	8,373,680	49,711	6/9/2004
Saskatchewan Prairie Shores Project	SK	88,775	88,775	201,000	289,775	378,550	1,900	9/10/2003
Saskatchewan Prairie Wetlands & Uplands	SK	246,240	246,240	167,200	413,440	659,680	5,100	6/9/2004
Western Boreal Forest Program	AB, BC, MB, NT, SK, YT	830,642	830,642	456,000	1,286,642	2,117,284	1,000,000	6/9/2004
Number of Projects: 31		$21,219,897	$21,219,897	$8,429,561	$29,649,458	$50,869,355	1,197,296	

Mexican Wetlands Conservation Proposals Approved by the Migratory Bird Conservation Commission For Fiscal Year 2004

Table Five

Project Name	State	NAWCA Grant ($)	Non-Fed $ Match	$ Total Partners	Total $ Cost	Total Acres	MBCC Approval
Acquiring Land Rights in the Northern Region of Calakmul	CAM	400,000	454,500	454,500	854,500	212,198	9/10/2003
Conservation in the Upper San Pedro River Watershed II	SON	116,150	335,960	335,960	452,110	69	9/10/2003
Implementation of a Strategy for Cons & Sust Devel Marismas Nacionales	NAY, SIN	119,800	372,623	372,623	492,423	0	3/3/2004
Integrated Conservation Strategy for Critical Wetlands in Quintana Roo	Q. ROO	163,683	205,000	205,000	368,683	0	3/3/2004
Participatory Ecological Restoration, Laguna de Sayula	JAL	198,967	199,647	199,647	398,613	0	3/3/2004
Protection & Management of Riparian Habitats on the Rio Sabinas	COAH	140,083	418,924	418,924	559,007	0	9/10/2003
Protection of the Rio Grande Delta, Laguna Madre & Laguna Morales	TAMPS	296,560	300,100	300,100	596,660	0	9/10/2003
Regionalization of the Pie II	SON	113,988	139,000	139,000	252,988	0	9/10/2003
Rest. of the Hydro - Biological Cycle in Laguna de Terminos I	CAM	458,880	642,570	642,570	1,101,450	0	9/10/2003
The 2003 Veracruz Model	JAL	70,000	90,633	90,633	160,633	0	9/10/2003
Use of Coastal Habitats by Shorebirds in the Yucatan Peninsula	YUC	67,800	149,150	149,150	216,950	0	9/10/2003
Wetland Cons. Corridor, Pacific Coastal Plain of Chiapas - Oaxaca II	CHIS, OAX	270,000	273,392	273,392	543,392	0	9/10/2003
Number of Projects: 12		$2,415,911	$3,581,499	$3,581,499	$5,997,410	212,267	

www.ingramcontent.com/pod-product-compliance
Lightning Source LLC
Chambersburg PA
CBHW052014280526
45793CB00005B/969